HOW TO STOP THE
BATTLE WITH YOUR
TEENAGER

HOW TO STOP THE BATTLE WITH YOUR TEENAGER

A Practical Guide to Solving Everyday Problems

Don Fleming, Ph.D.

WITH

Laurel J. Schmidt

PRENTICE HALL PRESS
NEW YORK   LONDON   TORONTO   SYDNEY   TOKYO

To Pamela,
my best friend,
greatest supporter,
and wife of twenty years,
with my deepest love.

Prentice Hall Press
Gulf + Western Building
One Gulf + Western Plaza
New York, New York 10023

Copyright © 1989 by Don Fleming, Ph.D.

PRENTICE HALL PRESS and colophon are registered
trademarks of Simon & Schuster Inc.

Library of Congress Cataloging-in-Publication Data

Fleming, Don.
    How to stop the battle with your teenager: a practical guide to
solving everyday problems / Don Fleming with Laurel J. Schmidt.—1st
ed.
        p.   cm.
    Bibliography: p.
    Includes index. v
    ISBN 0-13-435124-X:
    $9.95
    1. Parenting—United States.   2. Adolescence.   3. Discipline of
children—United States.   4. Teenagers—United States—Attitudes.
I. Schmidt, Laurel.   II. Title.
HQ755.8.F585   1989
649'.125—dc19   88-25437
                                                                      CIP

Designed by Stanley S. Drate/Folio Graphics Co. Inc.

Manufactured in the United States of America

10 9 8 7 6 5 4 3 2 1

FIRST EDITION

ACKNOWLEDGMENTS

As this book approaches completion, I am preparing to retire from the Julia Ann Singer Family Treatment Center in Los Angeles, where I spent twenty stimulating and challenging years as the coordinator of training. I want to offer special thanks to the director of the center, Dr. Susan Brown, who has been my friend and colleague all these years. Working with her has been a wonderful professional experience.

Once again I wish to thank my respected colleague and friend Dr. Frank Williams for his input and guidance.

Special thanks are owed to my wife, Pamela, for all the years during which she has been my greatest supporter and loving friend.

To Laurel Schmidt, my outstanding colleague who edited this manuscript and encouraged me throughout the project: May we write many books together.

I want to express my appreciation to PJ Dempsey, my editor at Prentice Hall Press, who made my life easier during the process of writing this book, and to Sherry Robb, my Los Angeles agent, who is my pal and insists that I keep writing so that we both can finally make some money.

CONTENTS

INTRODUCTION

Teenagers are a billion-dollar industry. Jordache knows exactly how to reach them. So does MTV. Television and music executives anticipate their moods and chart the trends while Madison Avenue pitches fodder designed for their mass consumption into a trough. And as experts are growing fat on the boom, the parents of these teenagers—convinced that aliens have taken up permanent residence in their homes—are ready to throw in the towel and concede defeat.

Adolescence is baffling, but help is at hand. *How to Stop the Battle with Your Teenager* is an antidote to parental despair. This book demystifies the rites of passage that characterize the teenage years. It shatters the notion that adolescence is a cruel invention designed to keep parents reaching for the aspirin and challenging the blood pressure meter to new heights. For those parents who think that the only plausible solution is congressional legislation outlawing the years from thirteen to eighteen, there *is* a remedy. The insights in this book, gathered from twenty-five years of experience, can change the lines of battle into lines of communication.

Perhaps after reading the title of this book, you opened it expecting to find an itemized list of weapons, lethal and otherwise, that you could purchase anonymously or assemble in your garage from spare auto parts. You might have expected the names and addresses of reliable boarding schools, all of them out of state and none allowing parental visits. Or perhaps you thought that there had been a sudden revival of interest in parenting techniques used in the Middle Ages.

A quick glance at the Contents shows that none of those items will be found in this book. Yet you are probably one of millions of parents who think that only measures that drastic could stop the battle that has been raging between you and your teenager.

You've tried arguing, weeping, begging, and screaming—that was on good days. Then you escalated to taking to your bed, acting hurt, and not speaking to your teenager. And after all that, the kid still scarcely seems to be affected. You may even think he or she is taking a crash course in "How to Drive Your Parents Crazy"—and getting an A!

Why This Book?

You may have turned to this book out of sheer desperation, thinking, What do I have to lose? Maybe somebody has better ideas than I do. This shows that you are a concerned, caring parent. But you need help. And one of the biggest problems for parents or teenagers is that there are very few books available that are designed to help with the day-to-day craziness of raising a normal teenager.

Yes, *normal* is the word for that half adult, half child who just last year was your baby. Suddenly he has blackheads, acne, and hates his body. Or is fascinated by it and can't stop looking in mirrors. Sometimes the kid you loved to be with openly wishes for other parents or no parents at all! He can tear apart the engine of a car but can't perform the simplest household chores, and he has trained his brain to work only when it suits his needs.

Or *normal* is the word for your daughter, who volunteers for every school activity, runs the political campaigns for all her friends with ability, enthusiasm, and success and is generally regarded as mature and responsible. However, at home she is overwhelmed by a simple request to do the dishes or pick up the dry cleaning and proves it by going into a self-induced catatonic state. This lasts precisely until the next phone call enlisting her help on the homecoming committee or for a project to save the whales, whereupon she is miraculously reanimated and flies out the door. At this point you may conclude that only a brain transplant will change your teenager's behavior.

This "normal" behavior can be abnormally difficult for you, the parents. And just when you need real help, the experts have stopped producing books. There are lots of books about parenting children in the preteen years. But the how-to-cope books for the after-twelves are scarce.

Many books on the teen years that are written for mental-health professionals give excellent and sometimes profound information about the developmental periods between twelve and eighteen. Other books are written for parents, explaining teenage behavior, suggesting methods of handling teenagers, and discussing special situations such as drug abuse. I recommend reading those books and have listed some of them in the For Further Reading section at the end of this book.

However, despite all their wonderful theoretical information about teenagers, these books don't help you with day-to-day problems. After reading them you may still think, What good does that do when the kid gives me those dirty looks? Theoretical information is important but does little to settle your stomach after a confrontation with your kid.

Many of the magazine articles you read about teenagers might come from literature about adolescents who have very serious problems. These articles also fail to help you with day-to-day problems, such as arguing with your teenager about the way his or her room is decorated with dirty laundry.

Either you are reading this because my previous book, *How to Stop the Battle with Your Child* was helpful and you want to prepare for your budding teenager, or that book didn't help at all and you want to give me one more chance.

This is the only book currently available that presents step-by-step methods for unlocking the struggle with your teenager. It is for the average family, whether single parent, intact, or blended. It is for parents who have read many books and still need help, and for parents who are locked into unending battles over such minor but significant issues as curfew, phone calls, and so on.

This book will also help the fortunate parents who have a good relationship with a teenager who is functioning well. It will be useful at times when you wonder how to handle certain attitudes and behaviors that you find disturbing, such as resistance to homework, moodiness, or speaking to you in a sarcastic, critical tone of voice.

To help you recognize behavior and attitudes that interfere with effective discipline, in the first chapter I will discuss the difference between your agenda and your teenager's. Chapter 1, "Disciplining

Your Teenager" presents methods that are simple, clear, and workable. Throughout the book I offer a serious but lighthearted perspective on the conflicts between you and your teenager in the belief that you can truly improve the quality of your relationship.

Other Parenting Methods

I have already stated that there are only a few books that deal specifically with the task of disciplining teenagers. These generally fall into the disciplinary-behavioral or permissive-feeling categories. Let's look at five approaches to disciplining teenagers to compare their values and drawbacks.

THE DEVELOPMENTAL APPROACH

This approach describes in a rather scientific way the stages that are part of normal development in the adolescent. These include social, emotional, and sexual development and attitudes. It gives parents and therapists a great understanding of what adolescence is. However, this approach does not tell you what to do about it. It's like telling you that you have a disease but not telling you how to cure it. Most of these books leave the parent wanting to make the kid read the book, or to hunt up the author and say, "What the hell good does this do me?"

THE DEMOCRATIC APPROACH

This method attempts to see the teenager as a rational being who can be dealt with reasonably at all times. It recommends a variety of techniques for talking to teenagers to help them discover ways of solving their own problems. A few teenagers actually respond to this method consistently, and it can work with any teenager occasionally. But if that were all it took to discipline a teenager, this book would never have been written and most professionals who work with adolescents would be out of business. Though the democratic method has value, it does not talk about setting limits. So its value is limited by the maturity of the child and the skills of the parent.

TOUGH DISCIPLINE

The disciplinary-behavioral or so-called tough love school of thought advocates an active system of interventions by parents, recommending strong confrontation and rule making. This approach was developed primarily for parents facing critical legal or medical crises with their teenagers. Parents are urged to establish their authority and demand strict compliance with their requests. This can be an effective "first aid" approach to a crisis; however, parents who use this approach with healthy teenagers are resorting to an unnecessarily authoritarian structure of parenting that does not promote mutual respect and understanding.

This method does not allow for adequate communication or expression of feeling by either the parent or the child. The focus of the problem is the teenager; the parents do not learn how to assess the impact of their own behavior on the situation. This is the main failure of books that focus exclusively on strong disciplinary approaches.

THE FEELING APPROACH

This is a natural extension of the permissive era in which many of us matured. The permissive approach emphasizes the expression of the teenager's and the parent's feelings above all else, and often at the expense of setting appropriate limits. The belief is that rational behavior will naturally grow out of this sharing of feelings.

The abilities to be sensitive, to listen, and to discuss feelings are all valuable skills for a parent. But these skills are useless if parents do not understand how to set limits on behavior and deal with annoying daily situations.

THE BEHAVIORAL APPROACH

This method suggests systematic rewards or punishments as a way of improving behavior. All behavioral approaches can be valuable in changing certain behaviors in teenagers. However, the problem with an exclusively behavioral approach is that it never teaches the parents to look at their own behavior. It also fails to assist the parent in understanding the teenager's feelings and reactions and is therefore limited in its ability to help parents act from a caring, understanding point of view.

SPECIAL-SITUATION APPROACH

There is another subcategory of books on the market that addresses special concerns of teenagers. Attention is focused on such critical issues as what to do when the teenager is drinking, how to handle gang or criminal involvement, or how to cope with a stepchild in a blended family. Other books attempt to reveal the personal hardships, confusion, and agonies associated with the teen years. These books are valuable for the depth in which they cover specific concerns, but they do not provide systematic steps for dealing with daily issues and problems.

The Job of Parenting

The current climate of the world makes raising teenagers a challenge. Changing family patterns, exposure to drugs, changing sexual practices, and the undesirable aspects of contemporary society make the task of parenting very difficult. Even when parents have been successful prior to their child's adolescence, they may encounter difficulties when puberty strikes. Suddenly the parents may feel that whatever they did in the past no longer works or applies.

If you haven't handled your child's behavior effectively prior to adolescence, then dealing with the teenager will be even more difficult. This means that you must learn new methods of communication and negotiation, and how to use effective behavioral consequences when your teenager doesn't respond to your requests.

You will also need to understand the importance of your own behavior and how it affects your teenager. *Changing your own behavior may be as important as changing your teenager's.* You will need to learn how to discipline and communicate in a focused, clear manner.

With teenagers, it is critical to learn to encourage their desire to cooperate with you. This means not only learning to understand your teenager's feelings but also using appropriate consequences when behavior is not acceptable.

Even though teenagers are a challenge to discipline, I believe that basically children want to get along with their parents and can develop appropriate values and attitudes. I have also seen in my clinical work that parents can be taught to see how they get locked into battles and learn how to unlock these negative situations.

How to Use This Book

As stated in my previous book, this step-by-step approach is not a prescription or recipe for relating to and disciplining your teenager.

This book is designed to give parents concrete ways to focus on specific problems that are presented by teenagers.

The sequence of steps, the consequences, and the dialogues are adaptable to your own needs. Some of the suggestions may not fit your situation or feel right to you. But I hope at least they will give you an idea of how to scale down the battle and present new ways to think about the relationship that you want.

If you find some of the ideas repetitious, it is intentional. I believe that it is necessary to practice these new approaches over and over in different situations until they become more natural to you.

How to Stop the Battle with Your Teenager provides practical strategies that work. Using this method, you can gain control of difficult situations, set firm limits, and teach your teenagers that they can be disciplined and still feel that you love them very much.

1

DISCIPLINING YOUR TEENAGER

"You're grounded for life!"

LOOKING AT INEFFECTIVE DISCIPLINE

As children get older, the challenge of disciplining them intensifies until, when the teen years finally arrive, many parents may find themselves living in the middle of a war zone. Teenagers seem to bring out the extremes of parent ineffectiveness. This is stated not to make you feel inadequate but only to acknowledge how frustrated you may become while trying to discipline your teenager.

When parents become exasperated, they resort to saying things like, "What's happened to you? You used to be so sweet. Just because you're fourteen doesn't mean you can talk to me disrespectfully. Or, "As long as you're living in this house, you will do what I tell you. When you're eighteen you can leave, and I'll even help you pack!"

The kid stomps into his or her room, slams the door, and doesn't come out for days. The parent turns to anyone who happens to be around and asks, "What did I do to deserve this?"

Exchanges like this go on year after year, with little chance of success. Parents keep acting this way although they know it's ineffective because they don't know what else to do.

Here are some of the best-known, most familiar ineffective communication techniques used with teenagers. They have never worked and never will, but they may make you feel good for a moment or two.

1

YOU'RE GROUNDED FOR LIFE!

This maneuver is used when you have had it with your teenager. It's designed to give you a moment of ultimate power, and it's usually said in a loud voice with your finger pointed toward the offender's room. What it really does is leave you feeling foolish, because you and your teenager both know you can't ground him or her forever.

OKAY, RUN YOUR OWN LIFE!

This is usually said in a tone of exasperation or indifference, conveying the message, "I don't care what you do" or, "I've tried my best, so let's see how well you do without me."

Usually your resolve lasts until the kid attempts to leave the house without informing you. You blurt out, "Where are you going?" and he or she retorts (with a look of triumph), "I thought you said I should run my own life." Again, you feel you can't win.

It's important to recognize that kids sometimes take your remarks literally, despite your intentions and then you are shocked by their response.

HOW CAN YOU TREAT ME LIKE THIS AFTER ALL I'VE DONE?

In this communication technique, the parent usually speaks in low tones and wears a sad, distant look. She (it is still most often the mother who uses this one) tries to seem utterly disinterested in the teenager while watching like a hawk for any sign of guilt.

Sorry, but by this age kids don't feel that guilty. They just get bugged. The failure of this method is that it attempts to discipline without being clear, hoping that the teenager's sense of remorse will do the job. If remorse worked that easily, the world would be a considerably different place, and the teenage years would lack their reputation for infamy.

I'M SENDING YOU TO BOARDING SCHOOL!

This approach is also known as "Help! I can't stand one more minute of this!" Unfortunately for you, instead of feeling threatened, your kid may say, "So send me. It'll probably be better than living here with you." Your response, "Okay, if you think we're so bad," only gets you the cold shoulder.

When parents make remarks or threats out of exasperation, they say things that they don't mean simply to have some impact on the teenager. However, their remarks rarely have the desired effect and may ultimately make them feel smaller than the kid.

YOU'RE NOT TOO OLD TO BE SPANKED!

Although parents sometimes make this statement out of sheer desperation, they don't usually try to make good on this threat. Even the most infuriated parent will usually be discouraged by the prospect of trying to manuever this adult-size opponent into a spanking position. If the threat is stated, the teenager will usually reply, "Go ahead. Let's see you do it. You can't hurt me!"

The parent then gets into a meaningless dialogue about learning respect, and the teenager walks away grumbling. All of this can lead to intense, angry feelings between you and your kid, and he or she probably won't talk to you for a week. (In some cases, the silence is an improvement over what preceded it.)

This section was not designed to make you feel stupid or ill suited for the task of parenting (though you may be saying, "It's too late for that!"). My intention is to illustrate those behavior patterns that parents are likely to get locked into. Until you are aware of what you are doing, there is no effective way to change your teenager's behavior. In order to assess how you are really communicating, you must be aware of what you verbalize and how it sounds.

In addition, you must evaluate your nonverbal communication (annoyed looks, the cold shoulder, or the laser-beam look, also known as the evil eye). You can probably name five thousand things your kid does that you don't like. However, when you are asked what you do to contribute to the discord, you will probably say, "Well, I hadn't thought about that."

To begin to understand how you are currently handling the discipline of your teenager, it is important to look at the reasons why you discipline. Surprisingly, the answer will not be the same for everyone, and the reason that you discipline will influence the manner in which you do it.

Why Parents Discipline

Now that we have looked at some types of ineffective discipline, you're probably wondering what *does* work. To understand what will work for you, we must first look at why you discipline your child and how you choose your style of discipline.

One reason parents discipline is out of concern for how the child is growing up and what he or she will become in later life. When a teenager is acting out and is unresponsive to discipline, parents sometimes imagine that the child's entire future is in jeopardy.

Second, you may discipline based on the example you received from your own parents. It may be the only method you know. Or you may be overreacting to the method you remember your parents using, so you have chosen to use tactics that are just the opposite of your parents'. If your parents raged or screamed in every situation, you may find that you do the same thing almost without thinking. Or you may refuse to raise your voice, even if the situation warrants it.

Many parents discipline out of anger and frustration. They only get firm with their offspring when they are feeling upset or are under stress. This is a particularly ineffective form of discipline, because your teenager learns more about your anger and frustration than about being responsible for his or her own behavior.

Understanding Agendas

To discipline effectively you must develop a better understanding of yourself and your teenager. This starts with examining the differences between your agenda and your teenager's. Agendas include values, expectations, and goals, and they describe what you hope to achieve or get from a given situation. Conflicts arise when you and your teenager view the identical situation with different needs, goals, and emotions. Constant quarreling between you and a seemingly difficult teenager may simply arise from a misunderstanding of agendas.

In general, the parents' agenda is to finish raising the child upon whom they have lavished years of patience, generosity, and love. They may have felt relatively successful at parenting until puberty struck. Then suddenly the kid who shared their interests and accepted their ideas and suggestions starts telling them that they are out of it, that they know nothing that is relevant to the twentieth century, and that their presence is barely tolerable. Parents view this as ungrateful behavior and a bad attitude. In fact, it is the result of the teenage agenda. The task of adolescence is to master the skills needed to become an adult. Its agenda is to grow up and learn about life. Unfortunately for parents, this is not accomplished by following the parents around and immitating their every move. Rather, it is done by testing, rejecting, exploring, and sometimes failing and then beginning the cycle again. It requires time, courage, and patience from both the parent and teenager. But it is the only way any of us become functional adults.

If your teenager could express his or her agenda to you, it might sound something like this: "Mom and Dad, you need to understand that I'm going through a developmental stage. Sometimes I need to act disgusting in order to be separate from you. The stage will pass, and you will like me again when I am eighteen."

If your kid said that, you'd probably have a heart attack. The point is that adolescence is a developmental phase that passes. The challenge for you is to learn not to take much of your teenager's behavior personally. I know that sounds difficult if not impossible. It's hard to accept negative remarks about your appearance, taste in clothing, and ability to drive from a fifteen-year-old and still retain your sense of humor. But I'm going to help you learn to react differently, so that you can unlock the struggle with your teenager.

Let's look at some of the specific items on the agenda of the adult and the teenager to identify potential areas of conflict.

THE ADULT AGENDA

Your agenda as the parent of a teenager is to implant values for adulthood. Your goal is to see that the values you cherish become embedded in your child's brain. You fear that if you don't do this now, the kid will never become the wonderful human you've been working to produce. Because your teenager's agenda is to test and reject many of your values, conflicts naturally arise.

Another parental agenda is to keep as much control as possible over the teenager. Parents fear the loss of control over the behavior, attitudes, and developing values of their child, although this is the reality of parenting growing children. So now we have a situation developing: The teenager wants less control, and the parent wants more control but feels less. Naturally this leads to growing tensions, causing the parent finally to resort to saying, "I'm your parent and don't you forget it!"

Parents also try to coach their teenagers in their choice of friends. Parents will often tell their teenagers that they don't pick friends well—that they can do better than the group they have chosen.

You are worried about the type of friends your teenager has chosen and how they might influence his or her behavior. Your agenda is to surround your teenager with people of good character and acceptable (your) values.

A teenager's agenda is totally different, concerned only with whether those friends are cool, cute, or fun. Their values? Those are their values!—nothing more, nothing less.

THE TEENAGER'S AGENDA

One of the most important issues on the teenager's agenda is to find things out in his or her own way. The years of experience and good advice offered by a parent won't substitute for the teenager's need to test what he or she feels about his or her own life. Sometimes this testing takes the form of rejecting your most cherished beliefs, such as religion, political persuasion, and the importance of the family. When choosing life-style and social values, the teenager is more likely to model him- or herself after peers or the parents of friends. Few things are more infuriating to a parent than to be told, "Jerry's mom and dad are so much cooler than you are."

Another important agenda of the teenager is to be accepted by friends. If your kid says, "God, Mom, you embarrassed me when you started laughing in front of my friends. Don't act so silly." Or, "Dad, stop trying to be so cool in front of my buddies, like you're one of my friends."

This behavior relates to teenagers' need to express their separateness and independence. They feel an intense need not to seem like your little kid. They may also want parents to conform to the image that they think is appropriate rather than accepting that parents are individuals, too.

Another important agenda of teenagers is to learn to weigh the relative importance of their values versus yours. For example, teenagers may be reluctant to look to the future because it scares them. Discussions of college, competition, employment, and finances can be frightening to anyone. Your teenager may act uninterested in what you have to say. Actually, he or she knows that what you have to say is valuable but just isn't ready to deal with the issues.

Another agenda you'll have to accept with a teenager is the need to outsmart you, to get around you. Try to understand this issue. Your teenager may say, "I'm going over to Jane's house." Maybe, if you're lucky, you find out that in reality your daughter is meeting her boyfriend.

The message a teenager sends with this behavior is, "I want to run my own life. You won't like the things that are important to me, so I'll just keep them secret from you. I'm going to do what I want."

Most teenagers don't step too far out of line, but they do do a lot of maneuvering. Throughout this book I will discuss how to deal with this, but it is important to keep in mind that this is normal behavior for an adolescent.

Defiance, negative attitudes, and rejection of your attempts at guidance are necessary parts of the normal, healthy adolescent's process of discovering how to grow up. Your teenager's job is to listen to you but to weigh and measure your words against what he or she learns about him- or herself and the world. As a parent your job is to understand your teenager and try to set up reasonable guidelines for growing up.

Observing Parental Behavior

I cannot emphasize enough that to deal effectively with your teenager you must first observe yourself. Observing your own behavior simply means *being as clear or clearer about your reaction to your teenager as you are about his or her reaction to you.* It means being very conscious of your moods and how they affect your kid's behavior. It means taking an extra moment to think of what you want from your teenager. Unless you become fully aware of your own parental style, you won't be aware of why the relationship isn't working.

Parents frequently fail to realize what a strong impact they are having on their teenagers. There are probably times when you feel you couldn't make an impact with a battering ram. But despite the appearance of indifference, your teenager feels and reacts to your behavior and attitudes.

As parents, you must learn that the intensity of your frustration and attitudes is deeply felt by your teenager. His or her response is frequently an accurate reflection of what you have expressed. For example, a parent says critically, "Your hair looks like you just walked through a hurricane." The kid turns and says in a nasty tone, "So, who asked for your opinion?" The parent says, "Don't you dare talk to me like that," never looking at the part his or her own attitude and tone may have played in the interaction.

In order to learn to become a better observer of your own behavior, think about this issue from an adult perspective. Suppose you haven't done something your spouse has asked you to do. She announces to you "Dammit, how many times do I have to ask you to pick up your shirts? You're driving me crazy!" It is likely that your response, whether verbalized or not, is along the lines of: "Why don't you sit on it? Stop telling me what to do!"

The person who initiates such an interaction (in this case, your spouse) is usually unaware of how much impact he or she has and how such an approach creates resistance in the other person. If you approach your teenager in the manner described above, you may get a variety of responses. A timid teenager may react to your negative behavior differently from a teenager who feels more powerful. He or she may not tell you or even clearly understand his or her feelings, but you can bet the reaction won't be very different from what your own would be. Questions you should ask yourself: How often do I praise instead of criticize? Do I take for granted the good things that my child does well without commenting on them? How often do I have to ask to get something done? If you ask more than twice without taking some action, you are teaching your teenager that he or she has the right to delay responding to your requests until it suits him or her. In this case, you should be aware that *you* are as much a part of the problem as he or she is.

Understandably, it isn't possible for parents to be aware of their behavior at all times, especially when they are struggling with a teenager. But if parents want to unlock the conflicts with their teenagers, they must become more aware of the importance of their own behavior.

Below are some parenting styles that will help you identify your own approach. I have concentrated on the negative methods in order to help you become more reflective—not to point out your deficiencies as a parent.

THE OVERCRITICAL PARENT

This parenting style is based on the premise that you can teach your teenagers about life by telling them everything they're doing wrong. All you teach a kid is to hate the sound of your voice and your opinion of him or her.

Usually you say things like, "You'll never amount to anything if you do things that way. You're so irresponsible. When will you learn to think? You can't learn anything if you do things that way."

Usually this parenting approach produces the most creative dirty looks ever devised by teenagers. In fact, I wouldn't doubt that some teenagers work on perfecting these looks in the mirror just to get back at you.

Many parents who use this style don't intend to be as harsh as they sound, but they are venting their sense of frustration. Parents who do this have either learned this style in their own background and/or they simply don't hear themselves clearly. Sadly, they lose any chance of having a positive impact on their teenagers, and they create intense negative feelings.

The negative feelings are not just directed toward the parent. Teenagers tend to hear and believe the critical things said about them. The critical messages become a part of their psychological makeup. The teenager who is repeatedly told that he is stupid has a difficult time believing in his ability to compete and succeed. A teenager who is made to feel helpless and fragile may have difficulty learning to trust and rely on herself. The greatest harm inflicted by the overly critical approach is the damage to the teenager's self-esteem.

THE ARGUMENTATIVE PARENT

This style of parenting puts you on the level of the teenager and demonstrates a loss of both verbal control and your own sense of authority. It is frequently the style of the least observant type of parents. Such parents don't see themselves as arguing. They think that they are teaching the teenager about life and values and feel that the teenager should understand this and not argue.

No matter how long or frequent or ineffective the arguments are, the parent keeps engaging in this pointless practice. The result is often ulcers or headaches for the arguer and considerable turmoil in the household.

THE PAL

This is the parenting style that many teenagers would vote for if you took a poll. Parents who are the teenager's pal are overly tolerant, demonstrate little or no authority, but are great for recreation and conversations. They accept most of the teenager's behavior without judgment and give kindly advice. This style is very common among divorced spouses, most often in fathers trying to deliver the "great weekend with Dad."

Sometimes your teenager will be good friends with a "pal" type of parent. You will hear, for example, how cool Mrs. Ackerman is. She's popular because she keeps secrets and never tells the other parents about their teenagers' inappropriate behavior. Teenagers relate well to this type of adult because the relationship makes them feel grown up, like a peer, brother, or sister.

Teenagers who experience this style of parenting learn most things the hard way. The overtolerance of parents leaves teenagers without any sense of boundaries or limits. They learn little about the important aspects of limits and controlling their own behavior.

THE ABSENT PARENT

This is usually a style adopted by parents who are professionally or socially very active. By choice or necessity, they are very busy and have little time to devote to parenting and disciplining a teenager. These people seem to hope that their teenagers will be mature enough to be responsible for themselves.

Some parents are in these situations by necessity. Single parents with limited resources frequently have to work long hours or may have two or three jobs. These parents have no choice but to encourage their children to become independent, responsible teenagers.

Parents who are absent by choice will often have other people care for their teenagers. They run the risk that their teenager will grow up without knowing how helpful adults can be in one's life. The teenager may believe that he or she can handle anything alone, or the reverse, that he or she will never be able to be independent.

Many teenagers who are parented like this tend to resent rules, reject structure, and find growing up difficult. If you are an absent parent, you may discover that on the rare occasions when you do try to discipline your teenager, he or she may have a hard time listening because he or she is not used to having you around.

THE AUTHORITARIAN PARENT

Also known as overcontrolling, this is the oldest parenting style of all. Basically the parent's message is: "I'm in charge, so you better watch your step."

Parents who have had very serious problems with teenagers feel a necessity to use this approach. However, even when it is needed or works, parents must realize that this method doesn't promote a positive attitude toward them.

This style of parenting is limited because it doesn't recognize the validity of the teenager's struggle for autonomy, nor does it acknowledge any of the other feelings he or she might have. Many parents use this approach to get control but damage their relationship with their teenager because the child always feels somewhat fearful and never really feels understood. Being overcontrolled can also cause a teenager to experience slower-than-normal social and emotional development.

THE OVERREACTOR

Parents whose style is to overreact are frequently at their wits' end. They are being driven crazy and life feels like one long nightmare, so they frequently resort to throwing verbal tantrums. What these parents really need is to go to their own room, or be grounded until they can regain control of their emotions. Seriously, if you have arrived at this point, no one needs to tell you that you have to get control of yourself. The way you behave is painful both for you and your teenager.

The overreactor needs the most help because the teenager has learned to tune out everything that is said and just sees the parent as an angry, frustrated person. Therefore, any positive influence the parent hopes to have is minimized.

If you recognized yourself in one or more of these styles, don't despair. It doesn't mean that you're an uncaring parent. It just shows that you're human, and it probably means that you need to become a better observer of your own behavior.

I want to state at this point that I have great regard for the parents who are struggling to deal with teenagers. The lighthearted comments in this book are not meant to trivialize your task but simply to keep your spirits up as you deal with the challenge of raising your teenager. More important, they are designed to help you reflect on your own behavior in a nondefensive way. In the next section I will present concepts and practices that can be helpful in changing ineffective parenting patterns.

UNLOCKING THE STRUGGLE BETWEEN PARENTS AND TEENAGERS

Parenting children is challenging. Parenting teenagers can seem like an Olympic decathlon. Each year (season, month, even day) reveals a new set of desires in the teenager and new worries for the parents. Even a teenager who rarely defies or causes concern will occasionally test limits, causing the exasperated parents to ask, "What can we do?"

Sometimes parents feel powerless in the face of willful and persistent adolescents, but their power can be restored through self-awareness and a change of approach. This section will discuss the skills and procedures needed to regain control of your situation and discipline effectively.

To become effective in dealing with your teenager, you will need to develop the ability to communicate clearly and the willingness to understand your teenager's feelings. You will need to learn ways to negotiate with your teenagers concerning what you want from them and what they want from themselves. Finally, you will need to learn the use of incentives and consequences.

This may sound as if you should sit down with your teenager after school, take the phone off the hook, and begin an intensive dialogue. In fact, it is much easier than that. The first step toward ending the battle with your teenager is simply to become more aware of yourself. Begin to observe your own behavior, moods, reactions, and patterns.

This is not a trick to reveal all your flaws. It is a way of focusing your attention on the person who has the real power to create positive changes—you! By observing your own behavior you will soon recognize the things you do that are helpful in solving problems, and you will also see the ways in which you may be making life more difficult for yourself. Being aware of your behavior can be the most powerful method of changing your interaction with your teenager.

FIRST STEP

Identify your parenting style by thinking about how you relate to your teenager. You need to realize that if you are relating in one of the ineffective ways described in the previous section, responsibility for the conflict lies as much with you as it does with your teenager.

After you have had an unsatisfactory interaction with your teenager, you need to think a great deal about what feelings you were having when this occurred. Were you acting out of frustration or anger? Were you just too tired to handle the situation calmly or to follow through? Don't beat up on yourself for losing your temper. At this point it is just important to try to understand what happened.

SECOND STEP

Accepting that your behavior plays an important part in your teenager's behavior is the second step in changing the situation between you. Remember how you react when someone talks to you with a negative or sarcastic tone, and try to be more conscious of your own attitude and tone of voice. When you are visibly upset with your teenager, he or she will respond to your looks and tone of voice more than to your words and what you are discussing.

If your goal is to get your teenager to listen to you, then it has to be done as much as possible when you are in control. You need to develop control of yourself and a clear idea of what you want from your teenager in order to expect a reasonable response.

You may find that you frequently feel frustrated in trying to deal with your teenager. This is because you have less control over his or her attitudes and behavior than in the past. If you are still using the approach that worked when the kid was ten, you're doomed to failure.

After challenging interactions with your teenager, rather than analyzing how your child acted, ask yourself how *you* handled the situation. Were you really concentrating on controlling yourself or only thinking about how your teenager was reacting? This will help you learn to see how your own behavior contributes to the battle.

THIRD STEP

Most disciplinary situations start out or end up being negative. Disciplining your teenager is difficult and can result in strong negative feelings on both sides. As a parent, you don't want these feelings to linger. You want to establish an understanding with your teenager rather than generate anger.

There is a way to diminish negative feelings and promote understanding. It is called *making a negative situation positive.* It is one of the most important concepts in this book.

Just because your teenager behaves in negative ways while trying to grow up doesn't mean you have a terrible kid. Most of the time you know that, but it's hard to keep it in mind when you are in the middle of a conflict. You can do this by searching for positive indicators within the negative situation. This is part of the process of making a negative situation positive.

To do this, you must learn to focus on the smallest positive change in your teenager's behavior, rather than expecting a totally new attitude. For example, you ask your teenager to clean his or her room. In the past your request would have been met by refusal or argument. This time the kid sighs and then does only an average job. He or she takes longer than you feel is necessary and doesn't have time to finish that day's homework.

You may say something like, "Look, you hardly cleaned your room at all, and you took so long that now you don't have time to do your homework. When are you going to learn?"

Then the teenager responds to your attitude by saying, "You always say I don't do anything right." He or she hasn't listened to your point at all but has clearly heard a negative message despite having made an effort to do what you asked.

Try a new approach. Say, "I appreciate that you cleaned your room. If you don't mind, could you clean this part a little better, and I think the rest will be fine." Don't talk about the homework. Accept the effort. Learn to make the negative situation positive by commenting on the effort itself rather than its effect or the teenager's attitude. This conveys the feeling that you recognize and appreciate the effort and that it is initially more important than the underlying attitude.

When you have been locked in a conflict with your teenager, this is where you must start. Once you gain better results, you can begin to work on the way he or she responds, which does have to do with attitude. In many sections of this book, I will show you how to do this in step-by-step procedures.

One example of working on attitude would be the following. After several weeks, you might say, "You're really doing a better job cleaning your room and I appreciate it. Do you think you could try not to act so frustrated when I ask you to do it? You really are doing better with your room, but that would help me a lot."

In this way the teenager receives positive reinforcement for his or her efforts and noncritical suggestions for improving attitudes.

FOURTH STEP

The final step in changing your approach is to make an attempt to be consistent. Professionals of all types—teachers, therapists, and others—tell parents to be consistent in discipline. The parents respond, "*You* try living with this kid for a week and then tell me to be consistent!"

Being consistent sounds very hard. If it means demanding the same behavior and following through every time a situation arises with your teenager, it sounds impossible. No one is that strong. Let's try for a more human definition. *Being consistent means disciplining your teenager only when you intend to follow through.*

If only parents would stop doing things like this: The mother shouts from the bathroom, "Get off the phone!" and then doesn't emerge from the shower for fifteen minutes. Or the parents babble over their shoulder as they leave for their own social event, "Clean your room and take out the trash!" Both of these requests were made without any intention of following through. The request is soon forgotten by you and your teenager.

You may be making requests and not following through because you are tired, too busy, or simply not observing your own behavior. You may be thinking, "Well, then there's no hope for me because I'm always tired and busy." So here is a suggestion that will help you become more consistent. Make fewer requests of your teenager, but when you do request something, follow through. In other words, instead of trying to discipline 100 percent of the time, discipline and follow through 50 percent of the time, but with these rules as your guidelines: Don't make requests when you are too busy to follow through. Don't make requests when you are too tired or not in the mood to follow through. Observe your own behavior when you make requests.

The secret is to enforce your expectations with enough regularity to convey to your kid that you mean what you say. If you make unrealistic requests that you will have difficulty enforcing, you are telling your kid that it's worth a try to resist or ignore you—that you will probably give in rather than pursue the issue. Some kids aren't even trying to test you; they have simply learned that they don't have to pay attention to you.

So remember, if you follow through 50 percent of the time and stop saying things the other 50 percent of the time, you will show your teenager that you are being consistent.

Once you have established that you are consistent, you may want to react when you are tired or busy in the following way: You could say, "I would like you to do your chores tonight, but if you don't, I'm going to let it go. That doesn't change the rules tomorrow. If you don't get your chores done tonight I will have to see that you do them tomorrow. I hope you can do them on your own, and I would really appreciate your effort, but I just can't do anything about it tonight."

This type of candor can be startling to a teenager and frequently produces most cooperative results.

Communication

As you begin to change your approach to discipline by observing yourself, you may notice a positive change in your teenager. You can increase this positive climate by learning to understand your teenager's feelings and becoming more empathetic. To understand your teenager's feelings you will need to reflect on your own teen years—what you went through, what hurt your feelings, how confused you felt. This will help you increase your awareness of how hard it is for your teenager to grow up. Being sensitive means accepting the idea that much of your teenager's negative behavior is related to the struggle to grow up.

Another fact to keep in mind is that it may be very difficult for teenagers to express their feelings in the most appropriate manner. To get a perspective on their struggle, think of the difficulty that adults sometimes experience in this same area. For example, a man comes home from work tired, discouraged, and needing emotional support. Instead of talking directly about his feelings and needs, he snarls at his wife, "Can't you keep the kids quiet?"

His wife doesn't have a clue about his feelings but is certain that she's been criticized. Her reaction is, Why does he act like such a jerk? My day hasn't exactly been a picnic. I've been at work too.

If adults always expressed their feelings appropriately, he might have said, "Gosh, it's great to be home because I had a really rough day." Or his wife might have recognized that he was feeling over-whelmed and offered to talk about it.

The point is that if we really reflect on our own interactions with each other, we will realize how difficult it is for all of us—adults and teenagers alike—to be clear about our own feelings and sensitive to the feelings of others. But learning to understand feelings and to be sensitive to them is the only way you will ultimately get your teenager to listen to you. All through the book you will find examples of empathetic ways of talking to your kids about their feelings while still disciplining in a clear and firm manner.

Negotiation

Some of you may already be thinking, "Negotiate? No way! If I give her an inch today, she'll be in Paris tomorrow with all my credit cards." Relax. Negotiation doesn't mean giving up appropriate con-trol. But it may mean giving up some of those long arguments and running battles that you have learned to enjoy.

The procedures suggested in the previous pages were designed to help you look at your own behavior as a new method of understanding how to discipline your teenager. I also discussed the importance of trying to understand your teenager's feelings. You may be experiencing some success and even having fewer battles. But so far, all the work has been on your part. Now I will discuss how to get your teenager involved in disciplinary issues through the process of negotiation.

Negotiation is the process of agreeing on something. It can mean solving a problem or acknowledging a difficulty. Sometimes negotiating with your teenager may feel like trying to strike an agreement between the United States and the Soviet Union before Glasnost! But negotia-tion is one of the most critical issues in parenting a teenager because teenagers want to be more grown-up. Through the process of negotia-tion teenagers have an opportunity to demonstrate whether they are as grown up as they think they are.

The techniques of negotiation encourage better behavior and attitudes through effective communication, problem solving, under-standing the teenager's feelings, and the systematic use of con-sequences when necessary.

Negotiation will call on all your skills as an observer, because you will be asked to listen to and evaluate your teenager's requests or ideas.

17

Your willingness to consider your teenager's approach to a problem lies at the heart of successful negotiation.

When your child was younger, you could negotiate with him or her through the use of behavior charts. Your child worked hard to get those silver stars or happy faces next to the chores you listed. I'm sorry to say that your teenager won't fall for this anymore. If you're desperate, try it—and please let me know if you have any success with this technique.

If you have been extremely frustrated with your teenager, then your negotiations have usually consisted of only one word: *No!* For example, your kid says, "Can I go to a party in Santa Barbara with the guys?" You reply, "No. That's the craziest thing I ever heard. And Jim drives like a maniac. You'll all end up dead."

Your teenager fumes, "You're so uncool. Most of the other parents didn't say anything about it. And how do *you* know how Jim drives?"

You assert yourself: "Don't get smart with me. The answer is no."

This is typical nonnegotiation, doomed from the start. You assume that the request is totally inappropriate and never consider the possibility that there may be a responsible way for him to go to Santa Barbara.

Negotiating on this issue might mean listening to the request and asking your teenager to outline a plan that would assure you that they would be careful and responsible. This might include allowing you to talk with the driver about your concerns, making telephone contact during the trip, or talking to the other parents. You would do this with the understanding that if your teenager acts responsibly, he will have opportunities for other trips. If not, his activities will be limited.

To begin to have a better understanding and less conflict with your teenager, you need to listen to his or her point of view and consider it *prior to* asking him or her to listen to you. Teenagers need to be heard not as little kids but as young people who have a point of view, even though they have had only limited life experiences.

Sometimes parents don't want to listen or attempt to negotiate because they fear that the teenager will try to talk them into something unacceptable or take advantage of them if they act reasonable. Negotiation is not an opportunity for your teenager to push you around or go on and on about personal needs. It is an opportunity to learn that adult behavior is not arbitrary: If you are reasonable, I can be reasonable. You have a point of view and so do I. We may not always agree, but we can talk about the situation and try to understand each other.

But good negotiation also means learning to put limits on your teenager's excessive demands. Most teenagers will be reasonable if the parent is fair but firm when necessary. With some kids, just the fact that you listen to them makes them feel better. This is the benefit of good communication.

I must caution you at this point that not all teenagers are ready for negotiation. You must be the judge. If your teenager demonstrates unrealistic or unacceptable ideas for solutions or an attitude and behavior that prove he or she can't negotiate in good faith, then the use of parental control and consequences is appropriate.

Like all the other techniques in this book, negotiation is achieved in stages that depend on your response to your teenager.

FIRST STEP

Choose a time when you feel calm and unhurried. I know that those times can be rare, but at least try for a few uninterrupted minutes during which you can set out the rules for negotiation. In a calm voice tell your teenager, "I know we've had some problems, and I'd like to see if we can find a better way to solve our differences. From now on, when we are discussing something that I want you to do or something that you want from me, I'm going to try to listen to your point of view. If you can come up with a workable solution, I'll try it your way for a few weeks. If you prove that you can get things done your way, and it's acceptable behavior, we'll keep doing it your way. This doesn't mean that I'll always agree with you, but I will consider your point of view."

This beginning approach gives your son or daughter a chance to feel more grown-up, to feel in some control over his or her life, and it gives him or her the opportunity to prove to you that he or she can be responsible.

SECOND STEP

Your teenager may come up with a reasonable solution that you are willing to try, but then can't or won't follow through. Don't denounce this as untrustworthiness or say, "I told you so!" If your teenager doesn't keep his or her part of the bargain, you need to issue a warning.

It would be fair to say, for instance, "You really started out well. But now you're not taking care of your responsibilities, so I'll give you one more chance to try it your way. I will wait until the end of next week to see if you can stick to our agreement. If not, I'll have to make other arrangements. I realize it isn't always easy, but if you want us to do things on your terms, you'll have to try harder."

In this way you acknowledge your teenager's effort and the difficulty of the task, keeping the tone of the relationship positive. But you also warn of consequences, which declares that you will take back control of the situation if necessary. This may be sufficient to correct the situation.

THIRD STEP

If, after your warning, your teenager still fails to come through on the negotiated arrangement, you must take back responsibility for the decision making.

You say, "I know this is hard to accept, but since you are unable to keep our agreement, you'll have to do things on my terms. If, in a couple of weeks, you seem to be listening to me without any problems, we can renegotiate and do things your way. And I really would prefer that."

When you say this, you give your teenager the message that you believe successful negotiation is possible and that it really would please you to do things his or her way.

However, if you have a teenager who begins to make agreements but never takes responsibility, never comes through, just resume control and don't renegotiate. If after a month or two your teenager reopens the subject, you can say that you are willing to try it again but if he or she is unable to act responsibly, you won't keep negotiating.

FOURTH STEP

The fourth step, which is an essential part of all successful discipline, is to give praise for any effort your teenager makes to honor the plan that has been negotiated. Most parents may praise too infrequently or too meagerly to build a positive climate. Their praise may be inconsistent, or they may praise only for certain things, such as good grades, but not for changes in behavior.

To become a better observer means noticing any positive change in behavior and praising your teenager for his or her efforts. For example, instead of saying, "Your promised to clean your room *before* dinner. Now you don't have time to do your homework," you might say, "I see you're cleaning your room and I appreciate that. I hope in the future you can plan your time so that you get your homework done too."

A parent might also say to the teenager, "Maybe I talk a lot about the things you don't do and I forget to mention the things you are doing really well. I'm going to try to tell you when I notice that you're doing things well and being responsible." If you do this, your kid may go into shock, but will probably feel very good about the relationship.

Remember that successful negotiation depends on your ability to observe yourself and on your teenager's ability to accept varying amounts of responsibility. If your teenager has clearly demonstrated that he or she is not ready for negotiation or if the negotiating process has failed several times, you will need to use consequences to get control of the situation. In the next section I will discuss four steps for determining and using appropriate consequences.

Consequences

Most of us would like to negotiate difficulties in a democratic manner, meaning that you tell your teenager what you would like and ask him or her to consider your point of view and really think about a good solution. You want your teenager to feel treated with understanding, and you want to encourage him or her to make personal choices.

We would all love to do this. It's a great idea, and with a certain type of teenager it actually works. However, with many other kids, you can't be that democratic. For, despite your best efforts and the efforts of your teenager, negotiating doesn't always work.

Democratic discipline assumes that kids can understand issues logically. Many teenagers who are great kids may not always be as reasonable as you would like them to be. When they feel very determined about what they want to do, they can be willful and persistent. Teenagers can also *talk* reasonably but *feel* unreasonable— their minds understand but their emotions disagree. That's when negotiations usually break down and consequences are necessary.

Using appropriate consequences helps you to feel in control and teach your teenager that it is still necessary to follow your rules. Many kids need to be deprived of something that is important to them before they will pay attention to your attempts to discipline. Sometimes even adults must be deprived of things they value before they can learn. I don't necessarily see that as a negative thing, it's simply a part of normal growth.

If you have been locked in a struggle with your teenager for a long time, you may have to start with consequences before you can move back to negotiation. If your teenager is very resistant to your attempts to discipline, he or she may need to feel that you are truly in charge and in control before being able to negotiate responsibly.

Here are the steps for determining and applying appropriate consequences for your teenager's behavior.

FIRST STEP

The first step is to determine meaningful consequences. To do this you need to ask yourself what matters, what is of value, to your teenager.

With younger children, consequences such as no story at bedtime or no dessert work very well. Obviously, it would be terrific if those tactics still worked, but unfortunately they have little meaning to a fifteen-year-old. But you might try them a few times just to see if they do work.

You have to be aware that as kids get older the meaning and impact of consequences change. Sending a thirteen-year-old to his or her room may be a very effective disciplinary techniquue. But by the time a kid is fifteen or sixteen, he or she wants to get away from you and may welcome the chance to hole up, have meals delivered, and see nothing of you. In this case, the consequence is not effective.

So let's look at the kinds of things that are important to kids as they get older as a guide to determining consequences. In general, the things that teenagers value most relate to their social world—either relationships or activities. Teenagers want to spend time with their friends and be involved in activities. Therefore, meaningful consequences would include not being able to participate in activities (meetings, school clubs, performances, sporting events); restricted use of the telephone; not being able to see friends, not going out on the weekends; and the limited use of television, radio, and computers. Any of these can be effective consequences for most teenagers.

However, individualizing consequences is one of the real challenges of disciplining teenagers. To be creative in the use of con-sequences, you need to think about the things that are most important to your teenager. The effectiveness of consequences de-pends entirely on the response of the person being disciplined.

For a teenager who is not very social, being deprived of computer time or the stereo can be a significant consequence, while to a gregarious child these would be meaningless. Nonparticipation in sports can be a very potent consequence for teenagers who are in-volved in athletics, so you may need to take away practice time or even playing in the next game to convince your teenager that you mean business. Another thing you can do with teenagers that you cannot do with younger children is to use an event or activity some weeks away as a potential consequence if behavior doesn't improve.

In determining relevant consequences, you should allow for the possibility of escalation. This means that you shouldn't start with the most drastic consequences first. Begin with something meaningful but reasonable, saving more serious options for occasions when there is no response to your requests.

However, if a teenager persistently and repeatedly acts in a negative way, parents must think about the most serious con-sequences. If a teenager refuses to follow the rules, is difficult all the time, and the issues are important enough, then it is time to take away something that is most important to that kid.

SECOND STEP

Once you have determined appropriate consequences for the occa-sions when your requests are not honored, you must learn to state in specific terms the behaviors you do expect. Your requests should describe what you want, when you want it, and the possible con-sequences if your teenager does not respond appropriately. Commu-nicating clearly gives your teenager fewer excuses for not responding and gives you a better idea of when consequences are needed.

Parents frequently say, "I told you to clean your room," or "When are you going to do your homework?" These are typical, nonspecific requests that your teenager immediately assigns to the category, "I'll do it when I feel like it."

In order to get your teenager to listen to and understand what you really expect, you should restate your requests in a form that is similar to the following statements:

"I want you to do your homework before you make one more call to your friends." Or, "I'll give you one more minute to tell your boyfriend to go home or I'll have to come and tell him myself. I prefer not to do that." Or, "Before you go out with your friends tonight you must do the dishes. I realize that you don't always like to do that, but that's my rule."

THIRD STEP

The third step will help you understand the value of patience and persistence. Being a good observer means being aware of how quickly you are ready to give up when your method doesn't work or to revert to one of your old styles of parenting, such as arguing.

Your reaction might be, "I don't care about a new approach. The kid just doesn't listen." In reality, the kid *is* listening and in many cases is responding. But the responses you see, which may be no change at all or even greater resistance, are evidence of a universal human truth. *Change is difficult, so people resist change.* Although we would prefer that it be different, the truth is that change doesn't come easily to teenagers or adults.

Thinking about how difficult it is to change behavior in adult relationships may help you to develop greater empathy for your teenager's task.

For example, how often have you asked your husband to come home at a decent hour and spend some time with the kids before they go to bed? Instead, he comes home late, overstimulates the kids, and makes them wild. You end up wishing that he would take a safari to Africa for a few years.

You have nagged, begged, cried, and screamed, but his behavior still hasn't changed. It isn't because your husband is trying to be willful. It isn't that he doesn't hear you. His behavior persists because his agenda is different from yours.

His agenda is: I don't get to see my kids that much, so when I come home late I want to play with them and they get a little excited. What's the big deal?

Your agenda is: I'm wiped out. I want my life to calm down now. I might even like to spend a little time talking to my husband before bedtime. Why does he do this to me?

Things don't change easily because the adult agendas are different. The same is true between adults and teenagers. Knowing that change will be difficult, you should be prepared for the following:

Your teenager's behavior might get worse before it gets better. This is especially true if you have tried new approaches before without success and are locked into a long-term struggle. Your teenager is basically going to think that any new expectations are unfair and resist the change, either through arguing or clever attempts to outmaneuver you.

When teenagers respond negatively to a new approach, it's common for parents to give up quickly rather than stick to the new technique. If you have been frustrated on many other occasions, your impatience could prevent you from sticking with an idea for the time it will take to succeed. Patience and persistence are key issues at this stage of the campaign.

Your teenager will resist. This resistance may not take the form of overt misbehavior. It may simply be passive noncooperation. "If I hold out long enough, they will change their minds and give up or just forget about the whole thing." This is usually right. Remember, if you haven't been clear and consistent in the past, your teenager will think that resisting is a worthwhile strategy. Even if you give in only 25 percent of the time, he or she will still feel ahead of the game.

Your teenager won't admit that your methods are working. Your kid is not going to turn to you and say, "Mom and Dad, I understand that you are doing this for my benefit and I agree that it's best for me." If this does happen you would probably conclude that you were having delusions or that your kid was seriously ill.

When you begin to use a new approach, your teenager probably thinks, "They must be reading another book on how to raise your kid, because they're acting weird again." Even if your teenager begins to make changes, he or she may cling to the belief that you will eventually abandon your approach. She will just bide her time and wait for your malady to pass.

Your teenager's attitude is not going to change quickly. Remember, some teenagers will show an immediate positive response to changes, but most will not show their approval. Think again of the difficulties of changing adult behavior. Even among mature adults change and growth require a great deal of conscious thought and effort. Treating your teenager honestly means acknowledging that he or she has the same right to struggle with these issues as you do.

FOURTH STEP

The fourth step involves evaluating your progress and making new plans when necessary. I feel that you must try a consequence for approximately two weeks to see if it is going to work, because it takes time for kids to adjust to what you expect.

The way you examine the results of a consequence is to ask yourself after a few weeks if there has been a change in your teenager's behavior. If you see no positive change in behavior or attitude, you must look carefully at the possibility of changing or increasing the consequence.

The big challenge for you will be learning to set limits without showing that you're upset. This means you must only discuss consequences and limits when you feel you're in control. For example, if you notice that you are feeling frustrated or impatient and your voice rises, you should tell your teenager, "I'm going to talk to you about this in a few minutes because I don't want to discuss it when I'm in an irritated mood." Discussing a difficult issue in a controlled, calm manner gives your teenager an opportunity to experience change without feeling a lot of negative feelings toward you.

Another important point is to learn to stick to one or two issues at a time. Don't try to discuss nineteen topics that bug you all in the same session. You will just overburden your teenager, increasing his or her resistance to you. Be observant and try to deal with one specific issue at a time.

Notice what seems to be working. Even if it is only a small move in the right direction, it can give you clues for expanding the process. If the procedure isn't working, try to analyze at what point you stopped observing your own behavior or where your teenager failed to comply. Go back to the last successful step.

If your teenager learns to respond well to the new method of discipline but occasionally has a difficult day, you might forego the consequences. You might say, "It's okay if you don't clean your room today. Maybe you need a little help. I'd be willing to do that because you have really been cooperating with me lately."

These are examples of encouragement and praise that can be used along with consequences to build a positive relationship as you carefully observe your teenager's improvement.

DIFFERENCES IN DISCIPLINING: PARENTS, RELATIVES, AND SIGNIFICANT OTHERS

While disciplining your teenager on a one-to-one basis can be challenging, sharing the task is even more difficult, for despite their best intentions, parents and other adults often undo each other's work. For a variety of reasons, spouses, relatives, boyfriends, girlfriends, and others fail to create a united front when dealing with a teenager. Some of the conflicts arise from the way responsibilities are divided, differing expectations about discipline, underlying hostility, and simple inattention.

As I stated earlier, your ability to observe yourself is a powerful tool in improving relationships. In this case, being a good observer means monitoring your interaction with either your spouse or others who are significantly involved with parenting your teenager to identify the areas of potential conflict. Let's look more carefully at some of the reasons why shared disciplining leads to problems.

UNEQUAL DIVISION OF DISCIPLINE

One of the most common reasons why people differ in their perceptions of the task of disciplining a teenager is that the task is frequently unevenly divided. One person does most of the parenting and the other observes. The person who isn't doing the daily disciplining really doesn't understand how difficult it is to be on the firing line with a teenager all the time.

To make matters worse, the teenager may act very differently with the adult who isn't parenting as much. Frequently one parent gets the best of the teenager, meaning that the teenager behaves better with the adult who parents the least.

The unobservant adult might see this difference as evidence of weakness or incompetence on the part of one parent. Being unobservant allows the less involved parent to say things like, "You're so hard on her. You're always yelling. No wonder she doesn't listen. You act like a child instead of a parent." And now for the big finish, "I don't have any trouble with her."

Suddenly the parent who has been trying to discipline the teenager is under attack from both sides. The first response is to act defensive or retaliate: "Why don't you trade places with me for a week and then open your big mouth!" Or, "Sure, you don't have trouble

27

with the kid. You're hardly ever home!" If the person being criticized is the father, he may retort, "Sure the kids are great with you—you're a lot nicer to them than you ever are with me!"

ROLE EXPECTATIONS

Sometimes parents disagree on methods of discipline because they feel that handling the kid is the other parent's job. Frequently the husband thinks that his wife should know when to discipline the kids and how to do it. Problems arise when she doesn't know what to do or asks him to take over some of the responsibility. He may refuse, knowing when he's well off, or respond by giving orders like a captain on the bridge, which may lead to mutiny by the crew (mother) and chaos below decks (teenager).

FANTASIES

Most husbands and wives have fantasies about what the other will want or be able to do in parenting the children. The wife's fantasy may go like this: My husband will be a strong authority figure and back me up. But the husband may have no interest in being involved in discipline problems.

The husband's fantasy is: My wife will know how to handle the kids, and I won't have any stress when I come home. Both are disappointed and even resentful when their fantasies turn out to be just that.

DIVERTING FEELINGS

Another important reason why parents disagree about discipline is that they choose to argue about their children when they are really arguing about their relationship with each other. Rather than confront their personal problems, they express their anger or unhappiness by disagreeing about how to handle their teenager.

LACK OF EDUCATION

Many parents have not been well educated about the effects of parental disagreement on children's behavior. When children, even teenagers, witness frequent conflicts between their parents, they may experience discomfort, anxiety, and concern. They worry about the

28

possibility of a divorce and may feel that they have to take sides, or they just feel angry at their parents for arguing about them. They may also become emotionally burdened because they are oversensitive to the feelings of the parent who seems to be on the losing side.

Teenagers who witness a great deal of parental conflict often lose respect for parents because of their inability to handle problems in a mature way. Teenagers are learning to be adults, and they look to their parents to model appropriate adult behavior and show how to handle problems effectively. When parents are frequently in conflict over discipline and other issues, teenagers learn that their parents don't handle important issues any better than they do.

INATTENTION

Some parents don't pay enough attention to the task of parenting, and so they fail to take care of normal disciplinary problems as they arise. When problems develop that require serious attention, they are surprised and annoyed and often blame their spouse for failing to take action. This leads to some major arguments.

Tackling the Problem

After thinking about the reasons why you and your partner may disagree and argue about parenting your teenager, try to identify the ways in which you express your disagreement. Many people just argue, yelling and screaming until they get the situation under control or someone gives in. But there are some people who hate fighting and refuse to raise their voices, so they choose more covert ways of expressing their disagreement.

Some people specialize in nonverbal messages when communicating their disapproval of the way their partner is disciplining their teenager. Shrugs, gestures, winks, grimaces, and smirks all indicate nonsupport for the other parent. When one parent is involved with the teenager, the other may shoot a look to the kid that says, "I know your dad gets nuts when you do something that he doesn't like. You'll just have to put up with it. That's what I do!"

Such seemingly innocent actions are far from harmless, for they undermine parental authority and keep the parents' frustration with each other alive and active. They also broadcast a lack of unity to the teenager, who will sometimes take advantage of the situation, thinking, "I'll just stay away from Dad since he's always overreacting. Mom is easier to deal with."

It is natural to want to lash out with harsh remarks when you feel your partner is not being supportive. It is also difficult to suppress gestures and expressions that show disagreement. However, both of these reactions must be avoided because they only escalate the anger or discord in the situation and divert attention from the issue of disciplining the teenager.

If you have fallen into a pattern of disagreeing about discipline, you can change it. Let's look at some positive ways of communicating that will promote mutual support and reduce stress between parents.

FIRST STEP

Take time to identify the areas in which each of you has difficulty with your teenager. Some issues may bother both parents while other issues bother only one. For example, your partner may not care about a messy room but may be outraged by lying. Understanding these differences will help you understand why you don't always get support.

To identify your particular areas of difficulty and the reasons why you disagree, ask yourself these questions:

1. Do you react mainly when you are under stress?
2. Did you grow up with different value systems about parenting that lock you into conflict about methods of disciplining?
3. Are you a person who tends to be judgmental about the way the other parent should behave?
4. Do you resent input from your partner if you are the parent who does most of the disciplining?
5. Do you think that your partner is basically too soft or hard on the kids?
6. Do you have a higher level of tolerance for a certain behavior than your partner does?

Those are some of the issues that can get in the way of mutual support and effective discipline. Take time to think about and discuss how you reacted to each other when difficult situations arose. Analyzing the roots of your disagreement will help you avoid similar situations in the future.

SECOND STEP

Once you identify areas where you both feel concern about your teenager's behavior or your behavior toward each other, it is important to consider that maybe you haven't been fair to each other. Admitting out loud that there are times when neither of you handles your teenager well is a good way to relieve a sense of blame or guilt that may have crept into your situation. This is the way you learn not to blame each other and to be supportive when one is having difficulty.

Maybe you are unable to accept your partner's method of disciplining your teenager simply because it is different from your way. No matter how right you think you are, you need to give your partner the right to handle your teenager differently if you can't agree on one method.

Let your teenager know that you may not always react to things in the same way but you respect and support each other. You might say to your teenager, "Your father has different rules than I do. He feels more strongly about grounding you when you lie to him. I don't always agree with him, but those are his rules and he loves you. You will have to accept that sometimes we do things differently."

THIRD STEP

Make an effort to stop arguing with each other about disciplining your teenager. Parents need to make firm agreements about how they will support each other's efforts to discipline and find nondestructive ways of handling differences of opinion. Following are two examples of ways to develop a supportive approach to disciplining your teenager. Notice that in both cases, the spouse is being supportive rather than critical and reinforces the mutual agreement about discipline.

The father says, "From now on, instead of blaming you when Anthony doesn't listen to you, and saying that you can't get him to do anything, I will support you by saying, 'Your mother has made a reasonable request but I see you're not listening to her.'"

If the father is talking to the teenager in an irritated tone, the mother can say, "You dad is starting to get upset because you're not doing what he asked you to do. I think you really ought to listen to him."

Another technique that can be helpful is to agree that if either parent notices that the other is not following through on a disciplinary technique they have agreed on, it may be mentioned in a positive, helpful way in front of the teenager. For example, "Do you really want to debate your expectations with Sheila?" or "It looks as if you are getting annoyed because Sheila is debating with you again."

Again, you are helping your spouse become aware of his or her behavior without being critical or nonsupportive. Don't take over the situation, force your own solution, or say that your spouse is a numbskull. Simply give cues about the agreement that the two of you have made.

Another method is to allow the parent who is disciplining to proceed without interference. After the issue is over, you might say, "Can we talk a little about what happened with Charles? It seems to me that you didn't resolve the issue and didn't really get your point across." After this discussion, both parents tell the teenager, "I'm sorry if we didn't listen to you very well. From now on we are going to try harder to listen and discuss things, but you have to stop getting so upset when we don't listen."

Your spouse lends support. "Your mom and I really want to learn to listen to you better, but I really want you to try not to get so upset when we don't."

This isn't the time to ask your teenager if he or she understands or to launch into a dissertation on your expectations. Just a thirty-second caring comment will do. When you respond like this, you teach your teenager that you are willing to take responsibility for your behavior, and you reinforce your request for changed behavior. It shows your desire to be fair. If your teenager is unresponsive or negative, you might say, "I know there are times when you aren't ready to listen to this, but I hope you will just think about it."

It's natural to want your teenager to respond to you, especially if you are trying to be understanding. However, change isn't easy. So you must try to accept his or her response, even if it isn't what you want.

Sometimes one parent unknowingly sabotages the discipline of the other. For example, Mom has just told her son that he can't watch football until his homework is done when Dad walks in and flips on the TV. The teenager seizes the opportunity, flops down, and asks, "What's the score?" Mom's natural reaction would be to say, "How did that TV get on? I told him no football and you are just letting him ignore what I said!" A better response would be to say, "I don't think Dad knows that I told you not to watch football until your homework is done."

When parents make advance agreements, this type of statement is heard as a cue rather than a criticism. The appropriate response from Dad would be, "Your mom is right. I didn't know you hadn't finished your homework. Finish up fast and we can watch the fourth quarter together. I know it's hard to miss the game, but your mom is right." Your teenager is given firm discipline and empathy with the struggle to comply.

It's natural for teenagers to go to one parent if they don't get their way with the other one. This behavior is particularly common with twelve- to fifteen-year-olds. As teenagers get older, they find this doesn't work and tend to do much less of this type of maneuver. If you have a teenager who does this a lot, you must follow up each time with, "Have you already asked your dad? What did he say?"

If the answer is, "Dad said it's okay" then you say that you'll give your answer as soon as you check with him. This gives your teenager the message that you won't accept his or her word at face value until the behavior has changed.

If your teenager says, "You never believe me! Why do you always check on me?" you reply, "I know it's frustrating to you when we do this, but until you stop trying to get around us, this is what we must do."

Even when you have agreements with your partner that are well thought out, they may seem artificial or they may not always work. You'll need to try them out and make adjustments until you find a system that works and feels comfortable. If you get discouraged in your effort to change the way you interact with your teenager, think about how well your previous system was working and how you miss those constant arguments that you had with the kids and your partner. If you think in these terms, you will probably agree that it is worth the effort to learn to relate and cooperate in a new way.

Separate Parenting

Up to this point I have been discussing strategies for parents who live together. However, because there are so many divorces, we must discuss the ways that parents can be supportive of each other even if they are parenting separately. You may be thinking that it's impossible to get cooperation to help your teenager. Not being able to live with both parents is hard on a child of any age. This should not be aggravated by constant arguing between the parents. Even though it sounds difficult, it is important for the two parents to put aside their personal feelings about each other and cooperate.

Typically, if one parent is having difficulty getting the teenager to do homework, finish chores, or be obedient, the other parent may say, "Well, he's no problem for me," or, "You just doesn't know how to handle him." This only frustrates the other parent and does nothing to solve the ongoing problem with the teenager.

Instead a parent might say, "I know that sometimes you don't listen to your dad as well as you listen to me. I really want you to try because dad needs your help. Let's talk about it when you come back from your dad's and see if you can do a bit better."

As hard as it may sound, being mutually supportive, even when you don't feel kindly toward each other, will help your teenager.

The Role of the Father

As I indicated in my previous book, *How to Stop the Battle with Your Child,* the father has a very significant role in parenting, even when children are very young. It is important to learn that a father can be nurturing and understanding, and it is a wonderful experience for a child to receive a father's attention.

But it is still very difficult to equalize parenting roles. Even though the majority of women are in the work force, there is still the ingrained idea that women are the primary parents or caregivers. Women tend to do more of the parenting even when they are working full time. But this is beginning to change; more fathers are getting involved in parenting, and I feel this is a very positive development. Fathers need to consider how important their influence and involvement can be to their child's development.

Parenting and growing up in the world today can be very stressful. Children and especially teenagers need the love and involvement of both parents, whether or not the family is intact.

Fathers need to understand that they have a critical role to play during the years when their teenager is preparing for adult life. As children get older, the parental roles need to equalize as much as possible because both the mother and the father have valuable skills and ideas to offer the teenager.

Children have usually had many opportunities to observe the

mother because she may have done much of the early parenting. But a teenager needs to see both parents functioning in the world. Therefore, fathers should try to give their teenagers some opportunities to participate in their lives. This may mean allowing them to sit in on a business meeting, spend a day at work together, or socialize with your adult friends occasionally.

This allows a teenager to observe the way the father relates to a variety of people, modeling appropriate behavior for a man. Most adults have the potential to model positive interactions with other adults.

Fathers need to be seen by their teenagers as people they can go to for help with problems, rather than just being the strong authority figures who create a sense of fear.

Ideally, a father should be seen as a person who can talk about his own feelings and be sensitive to the feelings of others. This may take some practice, but it is a valuable example for the teenager to emulate. Fathers should also share their thoughts and advice about life. Through this sharing, the teenager learns the value of both parents.

I encourage fathers to look at their role and think about the unique things that they have to share with their teenager. The value of a father's involvement cannot be overstated, and teenagers feel important and valuable when their dads are as involved as their moms.

Your Relatives' Role

If you are living with relatives and they participate in disciplining your teenager, you can adapt the techniques that I have just discussed to reduce disputes over disciplining. However, most relatives (including well-meaning grandparents) just drop in from time to time, bringing with them their ideas on appropriate behavior and discipline. Their ideas are frequently very different from yours, so they may be openly critical or just make faces and gestures that communicate their disapproval.

This does not have to cause conflict, but teenagers seem to have radar sensors that tell them when an ally or potential sympathizer is in the room. They may go into one of their routines and you begin to feel trapped or uneasy. Here are a number of suggestions to minimize problems between parents and relatives.

FIRST STEP

Let your relatives know that you appreciate their concern. Tell them that you realize they are only giving their advice because they care. This is a lot better than saying, "Keep your nose out of our business." Hostile remarks might make you feel better sometimes, but they don't produce understanding or improve the situation.

What you do is say to your relatives, *before* they visit, "I know that you don't always agree with the way I discipline the kids, but I would really appreciate it if you would try not to express your opinion in front of them. I want you to know that I love you and I love the kids, but I have to do things the way that feels best for me. I hope there won't be any hard feelings about this."

You might be thinking, "This guy is crazy. If I said that to my mother she would eat me alive!" I can understand your fears, particularly if you have parents who are extremely persistent, critical, opinionated, and have always had a great deal of control over you. It will be much harder for you to assert yourself so this approach won't completely solve your problems. But the following steps will help you get control of your own feelings and the reactions of your teenager.

SECOND STEP

Try to stop being defensive. You are probably feeling defensive just reading those words! How can you avoid being defensive when your mother delivers three critical remarks before she even takes off her coat? She tells you that the kids' music is too loud, their taste in clothing is terrible, and they don't ever call her. Your automatic response is, "You're always criticizing. Can't you ever say something nice about the kids?"

One of the ways to stop being defensive is to be much more realistic about your relatives. Be a good observer. If they have a pattern of saying critical things, prepare yourself for the idea that you will probably hear those things again and again for the rest of their lives, so you need to think of ways to handle the situation.

Think ahead. Say to yourself: This is their pattern. This is the way they are. They are going to say something critical. Don't fight and resist the idea, imagining or hoping that they will have changed into the sweet accepting relatives you always wanted. Resisting the reality of the way they are just upsets you. Accept it, but realize that if you are in charge, their words can't change your behavior. Your teenager is not going to say, "Hah! Grandma agrees with me, so I'm going to be a monster from now on."

The situation is upsetting but you need to remind yourself that feelings don't have any power over you unless you give them power.

You can also exert some power in the situation by confronting the critical or interfering relative in a number of nonprovocative ways. If you are a person who has a light manner of talking, you could say to your relatives when they arrive, "Okay, tell me all your complaints before we get started." If you can say this in a humorous rather than sarcastic tone of voice, you can diffuse some of the defensiveness and you may divert some of the criticism.

THIRD STEP

Shock your relatives and your teenager by saying in front of both of them, "Your grandmother has a right to her opinion, and I know she wants to help you. But even if she doesn't agree with me, these are our rules, and you will have to follow them." This is a lot better than saying, "Grandma, why don't you mind your own business?" and then, a month later, apologizing for being so rude.

FOURTH STEP

Knowing a grandparent's weakness or bias, a teenager will sometimes ask for items or privileges that you have already vetoed. Then you will hear the defense, "But Grandma said it was all right!" Your teenager needs to learn that the rules are not suspended just because you are out of sight. Tell your teenager that even if grandparents or relatives have different expectations from you, he or she is still expected to follow your rules and is responsible for keeping your agreement. No matter what the relatives say, if he or she goes against the rules there will be consequences.

Keep in mind that you may not find out what the kids are doing with their relatives. Grandparents sometimes like to have secrets with grandchildren, and relatives don't always understand the importance of your rules. If you find out after the fact that your teenager has ignored an agreement with you, confront the situation but don't make it into a federal case.

If a teenager has been cooperating most of the time, tell him or her you won't make an issue of it for that very reason. If the teenager has been irresponsible and has not been following the rules, then there should be a consequence to show him or her that the rules still stand.

You can avoid fighting with your relatives and having ugly scenes at family gatherings by placing the responsibility where it belongs—on your teenager. This is appropriate unless you have relatives who are influencing the teenager in extremely negative ways, such as involving him with drugs or other antisocial behavior. Then you need to confront the adults about their behavior and express your disapproval.

Stepparents and Significant Others

In a time when divorce is common, many parents find themselves raising their teenager with the help of a significant other person. This may be a stepparent, boyfriend, or girlfriend. If this is your situation you need to reconsider your attitude toward sharing the role of disciplinarian.

Do you have the attitude, These are my children so don't you dare discipline them? Or do you say, "I've never been able to handle him, maybe you can"? Or do you want to control certain issues and leave the rest up to the other adult?

It is very helpful in a close, meaningful relationship that adults work out arrangements for disciplining the children. There should be an agreement between the adults and they need to tell the children, especially teenagers, what that agreement is.

Some of the dialogue in this section may seem strange and even artificial to you. You will need to practice these techniques a few times before you begin to feel comfortable. Remember that the words themselves are only suggestions. It is the message that is important.

The message that you want to send to your teenager is that adults can agree on issues concerning the teenager and be mutually supportive and cooperative. Adults experience less stress when they work together on consistent goals, and teenagers will be more comfortable in this situation even if they don't act like it.

Differences between Age Groups

When dealing with issues of discipline for teenagers, it is important to understand some of the differences between younger and older teens.

THIRTEEN TO FIFTEEN

Younger teenagers can appear quite mature at times but will also have periods of regression. Sometimes they are able to communicate and negotiate in ways that seem to suggest that all your hard work is paying off. Your teenager is becoming easier to handle. Then suddenly the same kid can get as frustrated as a five-year-old. At this age it is still hard consistently to handle attitudes and emotions in an appropriate manner.

If you react to this frustration with your own frustration, your teenager will probably continue to behave like a five-year-old. I'm not saying this to criticize you, but merely to reemphasize the fact that your behavior has a great impact on the behavior of your teenager.

Young teenagers will negotiate with you as if they are fully grown and capable of anything they attempt. They will argue with great authority, trying to convince you that they can handle anything. You may see this as a sign of immaturity and think their demands are unrealistic.

In one sense this persistence is good because it indicates the teenagers' belief in themselves, yet they lack judgment concerning their actual abilities. No matter what parents say to them, they're going to believe in themselves and oppose the parent. Inevitably, this will cause conflicts.

A typical example is the fourteen-year-old who argues that she should be allowed to go on an overnight trip to a known teenage vacation spot with her sixteen-year-old friends. "Nothing will happen!" Or the physically mature thirteen-year-old boy who insists that he can drive your car if you will only let him.

It is very important for parents to understand the necessity of this process as a way that teenagers learn about themselves and the world. You can't convince your teenager that he or she is wrong about these issues; the need to believe that he or she is mature enough to handle life is very important.

Instead of trying to convince a teenager that he or she is wrong, the parents' stance should be, "I understand that you feel you are able to do these things, but I'm not comfortable with the idea of you doing them yet. This is one of the issues we don't agree on. You're going to have to accept that, even if it feels unfair."

FIFTEEN TO SEVENTEEN

Generally speaking, older teenagers have fewer regressive reactions than when they were younger. Still, they all have bad days and lose ground. But at this age they have a better grasp of what you want from them and a greater understanding of their own limitations.

This doesn't mean they accept everything. Some just get more clever at getting around you. Instead of having tantrums and being frustrated all the time, older teenagers will usually agree more, argue less, and develop sophisticated maneuvers to work around your objections and get what they want. They are not being liars, cheats, and manipulators. It is simply that as they begin to understand the world, they see that maneuvering works better than arguing, pleading, or having a tantrum.

You will recall that when I discussed teenage agendas, one of the biggest items was learning to get around you. This is more common among older teenagers simply because they have more autonomy and more options for fooling you and getting what they want.

They think like this: I want to go over to my girlfriend's house and then meet a bunch of friends to go out. I can't tell Mom because she doesn't want me to go out with those people. If I don't tell her, she will never know and I'll get to do what I want. This system works for me.

Some parents go bonkers when they find out what the kid is up to and act as if he or she were a bank robber on the side. This is because parents get scared when they feel that they're not in control. Sometimes going crazy will reestablish control temporarily, but it never works in a meaningful way.

Older teenagers are quieter about themselves. They keep their secrets to themselves. This is normal behavior, and they have little guilt about it. They shouldn't feel very guilty unless they are doing things that are very, very antisocial; then we hope that their conscience will bother them.

The older teenager will show less and less need of your company. You will be called upon less for advice, confiding, or companionship.

Understand that you should not take this personally. It is simply evidence that your child is becoming a separate adult.

Another characteristic of older teenagers is that they begin to see their parents in a more realistic way. This means they may criticize parental behavior in an adult manner, but they will also become more accepting of your limitations. Sometimes parents feel hurt, sensing that their teenager doesn't look up to them as much as before, but it is simply that older teenagers have a better understanding of issues in life and the world and a more realistic view of their parents in that world. Where there is a good parent-teenager relationship, the teenager's ability to accept the parent as an individual with strengths and weaknesses improves greatly as he or she gets older.

Last, older teenagers continue to need parental support and understanding as they move into adulthood, even if they show less need than when they were younger. Refusing to show reliance on parental support makes teenagers feel grown-up, but their need for support is still quite intense.

2

BEHAVIOR IN THE HOME

"There's an alien in the house!"

DAILY ROUTINES

Morning Rituals

Parents want desperately to believe that their teenager is old enough to start the day without a great deal of direction. They also think that their teenager is old enough to understand their expectations and comply without supervision or prodding. There is nothing wrong with these notions except that they usually lead to disappointment, because what teenagers understand and how they feel about it are totally different issues.

Once in awhile your teenager acts very mature, and for a week or two at a time there is no problem about getting up and getting going in the morning. This may lead you to believe that your teenager is truly on the road to becoming an adult. Unfortunately, the explanation is usually less dramatic and far less permanent. Your teenager probably just decided to get organized for a change but eventually will get bored with being so responsible and revert back to normal teenage behavior.

Another explanation for these sudden spurts of morning energy is that your teenager has developed a new "interest" at school and can't wait to get there. But if this emotional involvement fizzles out they may revert back to the attitude that the alarm clock is the enemy and school is the punishment. So much for maturity!

When children are young, they avoid starting the day by playing in their rooms and refusing to get dressed. Teenagers avoid getting started in the morning by staying in bed and tuning you out as much as possible. A teenager's agenda is to become invisible when called by pulling the covers up, hoping to be mistaken for a large uninteresting rock. With pillow clutched to head, teenagers are quite adept at shutting out all the sounds of the universe, particularly your voice.

Each morning when your teenager tries to pretend that both you and school no longer exist and when the camouflage routine with the covers fails, the big stall begins. In a whining tone or an irritated voice, one attempt after another is made to get rid of you, even for a moment. You may hear, "Leave me alone, I'll get up in a few minutes," "I'm tired," or "I don't feel well."

As a reasonable parent who has heard all this before, you say, "Look, I'm not going to tell you again. If you don't get up, I'm going to blow up that bed!" Your teenager screams that you will have to storm the room to get things moving, and then you both go bananas! The morning is off to a perfect start.

When you react like this, your teenager thinks that adults make big deals over nothing. If being an adult means acting like that, better to remain a kid and hide in bed. You must stop acting as if your teenager's life or yours is going to be ruined if he or she doesn't get up in the morning. Your nervous breakdown won't change your teenager's behavior, but the steps that follow may.

FIRST STEP

When you have time to talk to your teenager say, "I really want to stop being so annoyed when you don't get up for school in the morning." In this way you show that you are willing to take responsibility for your part in the issue. "I really understand that it's difficult to get up. I feel the same way about getting up more often than you know." This displays empathy and understanding for the teenager's feelings and behavior.

SECOND STEP

Tell your teenager, "We need to solve this problem, and I would prefer that you give me some ideas that will help you to get yourself up and ready in the morning." If your teenager has no ideas, tell him or her how you get yourself up in the morning, just as suggestions.

If your teenager comes up with some good ideas for changing this behavior, agree to try these suggestions for a few weeks to see if they work. It is important to be nonjudgmental about the suggestions. At the end of the week, discuss the situation again; you may need to give your teenager another chance. If you continue to have this same battle about getting up in the morning, move to the next step.

THIRD STEP

Tell your teenager, "Since you have no ideas for finding a way to get yourself up in the morning, or since you had difficulty sticking to our agreement, I'm going to suggest some ways I'll use to deal with this. I understand that you might not like what I'm going to do. I really would like you to solve this by yourself, but until this situation improves, we're going to be doing it my way." This statement defines your firm, understanding position but gives your teenager the right not to like your suggestions.

"From now on, I will ask you once or twice to get up. If you get up after I leave the room, we have no problem. I will come back in five minutes. If you are not up, I will calmly take the covers off you and put them on the chair. If you refuse to get up after that (within five minutes), I will leave the room and there will be consequences." Remember to use meaningful consequences and increase them each time the situation occurs.

If this action isn't effective, move on to step four.

FOURTH STEP

Tell your teenager, "You have to learn to get up when I ask you, and I really wish that you had taken care of this. Since consequences don't seem to be helping you get up in the morning, from now on I will call the school and tell them that you will be late because you refuse to get out of bed. I will let you be tardy and face the consequences at school." (This is called a mild social embarrassment.)

If your teenager wants to negotiate at this point, say, "Okay, let's see if you can take care of this so I don't have to call the school." Give him or her one chance, no more. Again, you are demonstrating your attempts to let your teenager have more control in the situation while showing that there is a limit to your willingness to negotiate.

FIFTH STEP

If your teenager does not respond to negotiation, or if mild social embarrassment doesn't work, move to the types of consequences that we have previously discussed, such as limiting the use of the car or restricting activities with friends. Remember! Effective consequences are meaningful, systematic, and slowly increased.

SIXTH STEP

If you have a teenager who has been very difficult over this issue and tends to manipulate you successfully, don't negotiate until you gain control. Move directly to the use of consequences until your teenager clearly sees that you are in control. Then, if your teenager improves, you can consider negotiation to help your teenager see that, with some effort he or she can have control over the situation.

SEVENTH STEP

When you have a difficult time with your teenager's morning behavior, it is only natural that you sometimes feel angry. You may fantasize about using a bulldozer to push the kid to school, bed and all! There is nothing wrong with keeping your fantasy, but an observant parent can learn to accept angry impulses and still act in an empathetic manner. Tell your teenager in an empathetic tone, "I know that I seem like a pain to you sometimes, but I know you can get ready for school if you try. I really don't want to have these disagreements with you because I still think you're a great kid, even if going through this makes us both feel lousy."

Telephone Behavior

"Get off that phone! Don't you have anything better to do? I'm installing a pay phone in the hall if you don't stop monopolizing the phone. I wish Alexander Graham Bell had never been born!" These are typical remarks of parents frustrated by the constant tug-of-war over the telephone.

Since many teenagers see the phone as a natural extension of their hand, it's hard for them realize that their dependency on this instrument is unnecessary and excessive. They greet their parents' objections with remarks like, "God, you're such a nag! I haven't talked to John for over an hour," or "Angie just broke up with her boyfriend and she *needs* me!"

Unconvinced, the parent screams, "Angie breaks up with someone twice a week. Get off that phone!"

Why does your teenager behave this way?

First, let's look at the teenager's agenda concerning the telephone. Girls, more than boys, tend to use the telephone to discuss in detail the important events of their lives—their boyfriends and girlfriends, parents and teachers. It is truly a way for them to learn to express intimate feelings and learn about relationships. Sometimes they are able to address issues on the phone that are too difficult to handle face to face.

Boys use the telephone in a slightly different way—until they get a girlfriend—generally to make appointments or discuss homework and sports, but they spend much less time socializing than girls. However, when they get a girlfriend, they may talk on the phone for hours, even if you haven't had a conversation with this kid in two years! He has a new agenda and it's called teenage love. We will discuss this issue later in the book.

Before you disconnect your phone for good or before you have one more screaming session, try the procedure that follows for changing telephone behavior.

FIRST STEP

If you're telling your teenager to get off the phone fifty-two times a day, remember to observe your own behavior. You must learn to be clear and specific about what you expect regarding the phone.

SECOND STEP

Think about these issues. Does your teenager's telephone behavior interfere with the ability to complete homework and chores? Is the phone monopolized to the extent that no one else in the family can make or receive calls without the operator breaking in? If not, think about why it bothers you so much. You may think that talking on the phone is just a waste of time. If that is your reason for being annoyed, you need to try to be more accepting of this behavior. It may help you to remember that this is how many teenagers learn about relationships.

You may be thinking, He hasn't heard the junk that they talk about endlessly. I think I'll puke if I hear one more wardrobe crisis discussed for the tenth time! Try to remember how important talking to your friends was when you were a teenager. If your teenager is basically responsible at home and at school but likes to talk on the phone for hours, you should be able to view this activity with a bit more tolerance.

THIRD STEP

If your teenager abuses phone privileges by neglecting other chores, skipping homework, or tying up the family phone for hours, use this approach: Say, "I have been thinking about how much you use the phone. I know that talking with your friends is really important to you, so I am going to stop getting so upset when you're on the phone too long. But we need to find a way for you to limit your time on the phone because it's interfering with your other responsibilities and no one else in the family can make calls."

If your teenager starts to argue, don't react in your usual way by raising your voice and enlarging the debate. Instead, say, "Either you talk this out with me without arguing or I will make the decision about how much you can use the phone without considering your point of view."

Remember, you are only going to consider the ideas that will help limit phone use or shorten the response rate when you ask your son or daughter to get off the phone. If your teenager has no ideas, or if those suggestions are not realistic, go directly to the Fifth Step.

FOURTH STEP

If your teenager comes up with a reasonable idea, say, "Okay, let's try it for a week and see if it works. We'll do it your way as long as you make a real effort to keep your word. If it doesn't work, I'm not going to get upset, and I will let you try for one more week. If that doesn't work, then I'll decide what the rules will be and let you know."

FIFTH STEP

Before discussing this issue, decide what your rules will be and what the consequences will be if your teenager ignores them. Say, "From now on, I will give you a one-minute warning when I need you to get off the phone." You must come back and check after one minute. If you wander off and get involved in other tasks, your teenager won't take you seriously, and the behavior will continue.

"If you don't get off immediately when I come back, you will not make or receive any calls for the rest of the day and the next day. If I have to keep telling you to get off the phone, or if you argue with me, the consequence will double each time until you show me you can follow the rules. I would rather not do this, and you will get more time on the phone if I see that you are really trying."

SIXTH STEP

If you see that your teenager is really making a sincere effort but regresses one day, don't get rigid and angry. Respond by saying, "Since you really have been trying, I'm not going to take another day from you, as long as you get back to following the rules tomorrow."

This decreases your teenager's resistance to the idea of rules because it shows that you can be flexible and reasonable if there is cooperation.

Remember, it all starts with observing your own behavior and taking your teenager's perspective into consideration. These steps can help relieve telephone problems in a way that feels positive for everyone, and you can break the cycle of endless, ineffective arguing.

Mealtime

Sharing a meal with most teenagers can thoroughly destroy the fantasy of the harmonious family dinner created by watching Ozzie and Harriet or the Beaver's family dine and chat together. In previous generations, when parents were more authoritarian, children either sat at the dinner table silently or were grilled on such interesting topics as school, homework, and chores. Teenagers stayed at the table whether they liked it or not. This gave a false sense of family togetherness and probably also explains the gloomy faces in many old photos of family dinners.

Some parents still value the tradition of family meals and have the attitude that "we're going to have a family dinner if it kills us." Many teenagers would prefer to eat in front of the television or alone in their rooms, so some of them respond to family meals by being disruptive or complaining bitterly about being forced to socialize with the family. Most can't wait to get away from the table.

Parents tend to be disturbed by this attitude, but let's look for a moment at the reality of the situation. First, the teenage agenda is that family meals are no longer as important as having a separate life. Parents have to learn not to be offended by this. It's another area where parents have to face the fact that their children are growing away from them.

Second, if the conversation is always dominated by adults or if the teenagers' ideas are not accepted as part of the conversation, teenagers may have good reasons to avoid family meals. Conversations that turn into inquisitions also discourage teenagers from sticking around. You can see them getting ready to leap up from the table as soon as Dad starts asking about the chores.

Observant parents avoid asking over and over, "How's school?" "Did you do your homework?" Teenagers usually respond to these questions with silence or grunts, which are immediately followed by, "Don't you have anything to say?" or "Don't be rude! Answer me when I talk to you." Your teenager is probably thinking, They always ask me the same dumb questions. I should make a list of answers and pass it out at mealtime. Part of this reaction is the natural need of teenagers to be autonomous of their parents. Answering questions about chores and homework makes them feel like little kids. And answering any question every night can become annoying. It's not surprising that teenagers aren't thrilled with the notion of the family dinner.

Other remarks that parents make are intended to teach manners. "Stop chewing so loud." "Look, you've got food all over the floor!" "Don't slouch." "You kids, knock off that arguing and stop interrupting your mother and me." Conversations like this only encourage flight from the table.

Yes, it may be a real challenge to get everyone together for family meals. When the conversation is boring or turns into an argument, you probably wonder if it's worth the effort. Let's look at some ways to encourage participation in family meals and make the experience more satisfying for everyone involved.

FIRST STEP

Think about what you want and can realistically expect concerning mealtime, based on your family values and schedules. Some families have no tradition of family meals, therefore little conflict arises in this area. For other families, dinners with every member present are an institution that may be threatened as teenagers develop their own lives and struggle for autonomy. Even families who really enjoy shared meals find that sometimes they must make adjustments to accommodate conflicting work schedules, athletic practice, and after-school activities.

SECOND STEP

Establish a family mealtime routine by negotiation or direct request. If it's important to you to have everyone present at dinner, negotiate. Ask your teenager how he or she feels about having meals with the family, giving him or her the right to express a preference. Prepare yourself for the possibility that he or she may not care about eating with the family. This is a natural part of the drive for autonomy.

However, if you feel strongly about the need for some family meals, tell your teenager, "I understand that you don't always want to eat with us, but I would really enjoy having some regular family meals. We are all busy people. We don't have as much time to talk as we used to, and the dinner table is a place where I can spend some time with you."

THIRD STEP

If you change the topics at the dinner table, you may change your teenager's attitude toward having dinner with the family. Tell your teenager, "I promise you that I won't use mealtimes to talk about your problems or question you about what you've been doing. I really hope we can find some interesting things to talk about." After you say this, your teenager may wonder if there's something wrong with you! This suspicion will persist until you demonstrate your change of attitude. Try this approach:

Learn to talk about the issues that are an important part of your teenager's world. If he or she is interested in sports, ballet, computers, or music, learn enough about the subject to show your knowledge and interest.

Be creative. Think about something you know or did that could be of interest to your teenager. For example, a parent can share a problem that occurred at work and explain how it was solved. This is different from just venting frustrations or complaining about the boss. It is a way for your teenager and other members of the family to learn more about one another and the various worlds in which they work. This doesn't need to be a long discussion; it's just a way of knowing more about family members.

Ask nonthreatening questions such as, "How is your friend Adriane?" "How is the school play going?" "Is your teacher still acting weird toward you?" If you ask with genuine interest and show a supportive attitude, mealtimes can take on a very different tone.

FOURTH STEP

Be patient if your teenager doesn't turn out to be a brilliant conversationalist after your initial attempts. If there is no response to your efforts right away, don't resort to old reactions: "Are you a deaf-mute? Do you have wax in your ears? Can't you answer me?" Instead say, "It's okay if you don't feel like talking. Sometimes I feel that way, too." If you behave in an accepting manner, your teenager's feelings about having meals with you will slowly change. Occasionally, teenagers need permission not be sociable because they're not adults yet. (Occasionally, even adults do.)

Behavior at the Table

Whether or not you have regular family meals, you may find that your teenager's table manners are becoming offensive. Your teenager may be a difficult and undesirable dinner companion, persistently arguing, interrupting, or disrupting the meal in some way. When this happens, you need to take a very firm stand.

FIRST STEP

Take a few minutes ahead of time to tell your teenager that there is a new rule concerning disruptive behavior at mealtime. If there are arguments or interruptions, there will be two reminders that such behavior is not acceptable—but no more than twice. If the kid can get control of him- or herself, fine. If not, he or she will have to leave the table and then let you know when it's time for another attempt at controlled behavior.

SECOND STEP

If your teenager doesn't try to return to the table, wait about five minutes and then reach out, saying, "I would really like you to try again because I want to have dinner with you. Please come back and try not to argue."

If your teenager doesn't respond, don't use the evil eye. Calmly say, "I guess you're not ready to try tonight, but I appreciate that you left the table when I asked you." In this way you are being firm but understanding, and you are reaching out to reconnect after the conflict.

THIRD STEP

Most teenagers won't carry this issue any further, so you will rarely need to suggest consequences beyond making them leave the table. However, if your teenager's negative behavior persists during most meals, you should talk with him or her alone before the meal. "I appreciate that you leave the table when I ask you, but if you don't learn to act differently during most meals, I will have to consider having you stay home on the weekend [or whatever consequence seems appropriate]. I am telling you ahead of time because I want to be fair to you. I hope I won't need to do that."

FOURTH STEP

Even if your teenager has changed only slightly, reinforce the effort by saying, "I see that you are trying and I appreciate that." Try not to be impatient. It may take some time, but if you follow these procedures, you will gain a sense of control over the situation and should reduce some of your stress. It also shows your teenager that you are in control.

Chores

When your kids were small and you first suggested doing chores, they probably thought it fun because it was something novel, like a new game. But after awhile the novelty wore off, and the game became tedious and boring.

If you haven't made chores a regular part of your child's upbringing, it will be very hard to introduce them in the teenage years. They may simply be seen as a punishment rather than increased responsibilities in the family. Even if chores *have* been a part of your child's routine, you may now hear threats about consulting the child labor board with demands for a hearing on unfair practices. Chores take time away from the exciting things in life, and so they are very unpopular.

Getting some teenagers to do chores may make parents feel that they are ruining their kids' lives. At the very mention of chores, many teenagers are transformed into slugs—spineless animals closely related to the land snail, which creeps along the ground scarcely moving. Doesn't that just about sum up your teenager's performance when you mention chores?

Chores are a part of being in a family. The parents' agenda concerning chores is to teach responsibility and to teach their teenagers to think about the needs of other people. These are important values for adult life, but getting your teenager to understand them and accept responsibility can be a difficult task.

Parents who have been very unclear and nonspecific about establishing a structure concerning their teenager's chores often resort to acting like a drill sergeant. The parent says, "Take out the trash now! Then I want you to clean up the dishes that you promised to do last night, and don't forget to feed the dog." Nonobservant parents will usually do this because they "have had it." They have decided that the teenager will do chores when told or face a lifetime of nothing but chores.

The teenager's response goes something like this: "What's the big deal? If you want the trash taken out so badly, why don't you take it out yourself?" The parent responds with, "Don't get smart with me or you'll be living in the trash," or some other meaningless threat. Although many parents don't say such things, they may feel a great sense of irritation and frustration. When parents become better observers of their own behavior, these dialogues will stop.

You probably wonder why the kid makes such a scene. Those chores should take fifteen minutes maximum. Try to remember that your teenager's life is so full of interesting events and activities that domestic chores could never be as important as they are to you! If your teenager had more awareness about this issue, you might hear, "Look, I'll get interested in this issue when I grow up. Really, I will."

Your perspective is: It's time this kid stopped acting like we owe him a living. Or, God, when will she grow up and take some responsibility? If you have been locked in a negative pattern with your teenager and frequently fall back on the timeworn comments that I have listed, you are just increasing your teenager's resistance to chores. Even if you are dealing with a teenager who is cooperative in many other ways, you may find that he or she has little interest in or motivation about doing chores. So let's see what we can do about this.

FIRST STEP

Begin by observing your own pattern of behavior. Notice the times when you ask your teenager to do chores. Choosing the time and the way that you discuss chores is crucial to your success. Don't ask your teenager about chores just as he or she is leaving to go out with friends unless you have a prior agreement that chores have to be done before going out. Don't ask about one chore while another is being done. Don't bark orders to do chores—no one is interested in barking except your dog. Try to use a reasonable tone of voice.

Be realistic about what chores you want done and be clear when you ask. "Take care of the kitchen" is unclear and leaves lots of room for interpretation. If you are disappointed with the results, your teenager can always say, "It looks fine to me!"

SECOND STEP

If you haven't been specific or clear enough about chores, negotiate a plan with your teenager. Tell your teenager, "We need to come up with an understanding about your chores. You need to try to do them more regularly, and I will try not to get so upset when you don't do them. I would like you to be part of the solution. If you can find some method for getting your chores done, I am willing to try your way and see if it works."

Again, over and over, you attempt to be fair by soliciting cooperation rather than just dictating the rules. This also gives your teenager a chance to solve his or her own problems and develop a sense of responsibility.

THIRD STEP

Be open to the idea that there are many systems for getting chores done. Your teenager may come up with a good one that suits his personality and schedule. If your teenager thinks of a good solution, say "I think your suggestion is reasonable. We'll try it your way for a month. If your system doesn't work, then you'll have to do your chores when I say they must be done. I will consider the possibility of renegotiating after you have been responsible about your chores for a few months."

If a systematic approach doesn't work and your teenager has proven that she is unable to act responsibly, don't keep giving chances, just take control. You should say, "I think it would make you feel better if you would be responsible for your chores and didn't have to do it my way. I hope you will consider that." In this way you try to help your teenager see that cooperative behavior is to her benefit.

FOURTH STEP

If your teenager refuses to follow these rules or take responsibility, simply say that the chores must be done now. No excuses! Gently take the kid's arm and say supportively, "Let's get this thing done." This means that no matter what he or she is doing, chores come first. As soon as they are finished, your teenager can do whatever was planned. In this way you don't need a consequence, just control over getting what you expect.

Remember, when you get to this point it will be necessary to stay near your teenager until the jobs are completed. Rather than harp on what hasn't been done or what has been missed, it may help to say calmly and firmly, "Let's get this out of the way so you can do what you want." Remember, let nothing distract you from this disciplining.

Finally, say to your teenager, "Look, I know that this really bugs you, but once your chores are out of the way we get along better and you get to go out." When you start handling issues like this, your teenager may wonder if you are well because the interaction will feel so different. This technique, which can work with most teenagers, really increases the potential of your teenager cooperating with you.

However, if your teenager is extremely resistant, you will need to use consequences.

Homework

Even if your child had problems with homework in elementary school, you may think that as a teenager he or she will be mature enough to be responsible for doing homework without much direction from you. However, that's just a nice fantasy. It is more likely that you will see a person propped up in front of a pile of books, in an apparent comatose state.

You say, "What are you doing? Why aren't you doing your homework? Remember, you're getting older and this counts for college!" You have failed to note that *comatose* means lack of alertness, inertness, abnormal drowsiness, and a quality of laziness or indifference!

After your teenager is brought back to life by your shouting, you proceed with comments such as, "I'm only telling you these things for your own good." Remarks like this are the result of the parent's fear that the teenager's present behavior foretells the future. That fear includes the concern that if the teenager doesn't learn to be responsible about homework, he or she will be living at home permanently.

As you become more worried about your child's potential failure, and more frustrated, you may experience a mild form of insanity. The symptoms include screaming at your spouse (who has no homework), ripping the cord from the television set, and threatening to send your teenager to boarding school in Siberia.

In desperation, you may throw up your hands and say, "All right, I'll never say another word to you about your homework. It's your life. Ruin it if you want!" Your teenager thinks that you have finally given up and is relieved to have you off the case.

Of course, no responsible parent could keep a promise like that, so the next day you increase the threats and dire predictions. "If you don't do your homework, you'll never leave this house again!" If you recognize these symptoms in yourself, you have temporary homework-induced insanity, and you should read the next section carefully.

Let's talk for a moment about how your teenager sees homework. Your teenager is struggling with the fact that homework is an unavoidable daily responsibility. Parents need to remember from their own experience that it's difficult during adolescence to do anything that consistently. It's just not easy to be responsible for such a long period of time. Therefore, most teenagers struggle with homework from time to time. Few teenagers sit down every day and do their homework without resistance. When kids do act like that, parents often think they have a rare studying disease that should not be cured. In other words, resisting homework is a fairly normal teenage reaction.

Many teenagers view homework as a mandatory, long-term sentence without possibility of parole, and they are always trying to escape. Homework is often boring and frustrating, so teenagers try to combat the discomfort by watching television, listening to the radio, getting up and down, or just spacing out. A favorite avoidance technique of teenagers (and some adults) is to wait until the last moment to start their homework, then panic, ask for help, stay up all night, and finally get it done.

Parents should realize that taking responsibility for homework is a developmental issue for teenagers. It's the beginning of learning to work consistently. Because it is difficult for teenagers to want to learn this skill, parents need to discover how to help them deal with their discomfort.

FIRST STEP

First, observe yourself to see how often you nag, argue, yell at, or criticize your teenager about homework. Being more observant means developing an awareness of the feelings that lead you to yell or nag. Parents usually nag or yell because they feel helpless in their attempts to get their teenagers to study. Being more observant means saying to yourself, I know this doesn't work, and I must try to get better control of my reactions.

SECOND STEP

In as calm a manner as possible, tell your teenager that you understand how natural it is to want to avoid doing homework. You also realize that nagging doesn't help the situation, and you will really try not to do it anymore. Perhaps both of you can come up with some different ways to handle the homework problem.

THIRD STEP

If you have a teenager who gets good grades and is basically a good student but who doesn't appear to be well organized or always does homework at the last minute, you should say something like this: "I don't tell you often enough that I know you are a good student and that I am proud of you. Sometimes you might think that because I nag you about homework, I don't appreciate how well you do. But I do.

"But you really need to be more organized and not wait until the last minute to do your homework. I realize that you don't think that's very important now, but later in your life it will be, and I am trying to help you learn that now."

FOURTH STEP

If your teenager is responsible in most areas except homework, it is likely that he or she will be a responsible adult. Say that you want to negotiate a better structure for getting homework done. Ask your teenager to think about what would work, or to think of several different plans depending on work or practice schedules. Follow up after a week to evaluate the success of the new plans.

If your teenager has not found a plan, suggest one that must be tried. One system would be to do homework at the same time each day. No excuses!

FIFTH STEP

If you have tried all of the above with your teenager and the homework is still not being completed in a consistent, orderly fashion, you will need to take more control. This will also be necessary when dealing with a teenager who has always had problems completing homework. Say, "Since you are not able to find a homework system that works for you, I will set the rules about homework. Your homework time will be after school/after dinner, and you may not watch television or talk on the phone with your friends until it is done. No exceptions."

SIXTH STEP

Teenagers who really dislike homework sometimes try to escape the dreary task by acting as if it doesn't exist. To do this successfully, they must also convince their parents who are usually suspicious. "Do you mean to tell me that your history teacher hasn't assigned homework in two weeks? I know her. She never forgets homework!" The teenager will usually shrug and mumble, "I told you I don't have any home-work. Why do you keep asking me?"

If your teenager consistently denies having any homework, you should say, "It seems that you have a hard time telling me the truth about your homework. If I find out that you didn't tell me the truth, there will be consequences until you learn to be honest. I hope you will tell me the truth so that won't happen." Again, you demonstrate your goodwill while being firm.

SEVENTH STEP

In dealing with difficult homework problems, it is often helpful to enlist the aid of your teenager's teachers. Teachers usually assign homework on specific days and are happy to tell you their schedule. They also welcome parental support in teaching students to be responsible about homework. If you talk to them about your concerns and plans for action, they are usually glad to cooperate.

Tell your teenager that until he or she learns to be more responsible about doing homework, you will expect a signed note from each teacher at the end of each week, listing the assignments for that week. It is a good idea to call the teachers to explain your system and ask for their assistance. If your request is specific and simple, most teachers will follow through.

If your teenager refuses to cooperate, introduce a consequence. An appropriate consequence might be losing one day of weekend activities. If your teenager persists in being irresponsible, you persist by increasing the consequences to two days at a time and so on, until your teenager realizes that the consequences are more inconvenient that simply doing the homework.

Once you show that you're in control and that your teenager can't get around you anymore, he or she will find the resources to become more responsible.

EIGHTH STEP

Let your teenager know that you understand, that you realize this is a difficult issue, and that it is hard to do homework every night. You know that some nights will be easier than others, and you realize that the kid's moods will go up and down. Tell your teenager that you intend to be firm about homework, but you will also try to be more patient.

Bedtime

Bedtime raises the same objections from small children and teenagers: They just don't want to go to bed when you tell them! Younger children say they are afraid of the dark or they're thirsty or hungry. They try to come out of their rooms or get you to come in and keep them company because they simply don't want to go to bed. Teenagers just want to stay in their rooms, have some privacy, and be left alone until they are ready to go to bed.

In reality, this is a minor problem compared to some of the other issues that you will face in raising your teenager. Yet, some parents find themselves making comments and having arguments until bedtime becomes a major issue. They say, "Get to bed, turn out that light! Didn't I tell you to get to sleep an hour ago?" The teenager retorts, "I'm not tired. Why can't I stay up longer?"

The teenager's view of bedtime is considerably different from the adult's. Bedtime is something adults long for after a full day of work and family responsibilities. A teenager sees the late evening as a time to stay up and be left alone.

It is important for tired parents to remember that most teenagers have so much energy that their erratic sleeping patterns and insufficient sleep rarely create any major problems. Exceptions are teenagers who always stay up late to do homework and can't wake up easily, or those who just stay up late and then refuse to get out of bed in the morning.

Since there are so many other issues for which teenagers can't assume control, let them take as much responsibility as possible for the pattern of their bedtime. Only make an issue of bedtime if you can substantiate your feeling that your teenager is not functioning well because of unhealthy bedtime patterns. If you feel that the hours your teenager is keeping are causing problems, try the steps that follow.

FIRST STEP

You need to ask youself if you react to your teenager's nighttime patterns in very unobservant ways. Do you periodically make negative or judgmental comments about your teenager's bedtime without clarifying what you expect in place of the current behavior? Do you feel annoyed by the fact that your teenager stays up late, even if there are no problems caused by the late hour? Do you think that he or she is just wasting time? Maybe your reaction is simply left over from all those years of having to enforce bedtime for younger children.

SECOND STEP

Negotiate a specific understanding with your teenager, such as, "As long as you act responsibly about schoolwork and getting up in the morning, I will leave your bedtime up to you. But if I see that you are overtired and can't function well, then I'll expect you to think about an alternate bedtime schedule until you get back in control of your responsibilities."

Teenagers Spending Time in Their Rooms

Beginning around the age of fifteen, some teenagers literally hibernate in their rooms for a number of years. The same kid who always wanted to spend time with the family suddenly disappears behind the door of his or her room for such long periods that the parents begin to wonder if he or she will ever return. (Depending on how you get along with your teenager, you might welcome and even encourage this behavior!)

A teenager's room is a private domain. It's the one place where the kid can be alone, autonomous, and feel totally in control. In this small world anything is possible without the risk of failure or criticism.

Alone in their rooms, teenagers like to listen to music, talk on the telephone, or write in a diary. Some of their stranger pastimes include looking at themselves in the mirror for hours. Face watching is very important to teenagers because they are hoping that any imperfections will magically change just by staring long enough. This behavior may also be common in the bathroom, causing shrieks of protest from other family members who are waiting to get in. Although this may seem strange to parents, it is related to the normal teenage preoccupation with self-image.

Teenagers also use their rooms as private places where they can work out such feelings as anger, hurt, or sadness on their own. By being physically separate, the teenager is learning to handle personal feelings without always relying on you for help, comments, or advice.

The parent's reaction to teenage hibernation may include feelings of confusion, concern, and even a sense of rejection. Why is my kid withdrawing? Is he in trouble? Is something wrong? Did I say something? Did I miss something? I hate it when she just stays in her room! Let's look at some ways of making this issue more understand-able and comfortable for parents.

FIRST STEP

Begin to observe your own behavior. Pay attention to the feelings you have when your teenager stays in his or her room for a long time. Doing so will help you discover why this behavior bothers you. For example, do you take it personally that the kid wants to spend so much time away from you? Do you feel that your teenager is hiding out to avoid responsibilities? Do you think she is just wasting time? Do you worry that it means he's on drugs or depressed? It's important for parents to understand that in most cases this need to be alone is just part of normal development, and it will change.

SECOND STEP

Observe the things you say on this issue. Are you conveying the message that you have negative feelings about the amount of time your teenager spends in his or her room? For example, do you say things like, "Why do you spend so much time in your room? All you do is go in and talk on the phone for hours! You're so unfriendly lately! You'd rather be in your room than spend any time with us"?

Most parents react this way because they are confused and don't know what to think about this withdrawing behavior. Your teenager can't answer your questions in a way that reassures you, and your comments and probing may just create more negative feelings.

THIRD STEP

Say to your teenager, "Look, I really will try to stop asking you why you spend so much time in your room. I realize that it's one of the few places that you can be alone and feel that no one's going to bother you. I know that sometimes you go in your room because you're upset with us, and I hope that you will try to tell us so we can work out the problem."

FOURTH STEP

Being understanding about your teenager's need for solitude doesn't mean that you have to lose contact for years. You can respect his or her privacy and still initiate conversations and spend time together.

If you feel the need to spend more time with your teenager, you might say, "Honey, sometimes I would like to invite myself into your room just to talk a little more than we have lately. However, anytime you don't want to talk when you're in your room, I want you to know that it's okay. Just tell me and I won't be offended."

Leaving Personal Items around the House

Teenagers walk through the house, randomly dropping clothes, books, and other items as if the entire place were their personal storage bin. Towels on the toaster, shoes on the television. No area of the house is sacred! Teenagers are oblivious to anyone or anything in their path. This phenomenon may be said to resemble a strange disease that suddenly appears between the ages of thirteen and eighteen and then disappears just as abruptly.

Few parents are willing to accept this diagnosis, however. They simply conclude that their kid is a slob. He or she is slovenly, inconsiderate, and a real pain! Let's see if you can understand the teenager's point of view and learn ways to encourage more responsible behavior in your teenager.

Teenagers basically don't see the same need for orderliness that their parents seem to cherish. Since they don't need order in their physical surroundings, they are puzzled when their parents harp on tidying up, cleaning, and being organized. Why *not* throw underwear behind the bed?!

Part of growing up is learning to develop an internal need for structure. This sense of order usually comes later in life when the young adult gets that first apartment or place that's all his or her own. Until then most young adults feel like a kid in Mom and Dad's house. Another aspect of growing up is developing an awareness of other people's needs. Both of these are lifelong tasks that the teenager is just beginning to learn.

Most teenagers are only concerned about orderliness when their personal or social lives are threatened. Getting ready for school or leaving for athletic practice, your teenager may shout, "Where are my shoes? Has anyone seen my jacket?" Seizing the opportunity to advance your campaign for orderliness, you reply, "It's no wonder you can't find anything when you scatter things from one end of the house to the other. Then you expect your clothes to appear magically when you need them. Do you think I exist simply to help you locate the things you've lost?" Your teenager snarls, "Fine, don't help me. I'll go barefoot!"

There's a way to end these meaningless dialogues and help you feel less frustrated.

FIRST STEP

Have you been nagging your teenager about untidiness, yet picking up his or her things or throwing everything into his or her room? Tell your teenager, "Its unrealistic for me to get upset when you don't pick up your clothes and other things if I have never really told you what I need and expect of you." This shows your teenager that you're not blaming him or her for the current situation. You take responsibility for not being clear, and at the same time you let your kid know that things are about to change.

SECOND STEP

Tell your teenager, "I need you to think of a way to get more organized about picking up your belongings. It has to be done, but you can figure out your own system. I want you to decide how I can remind you in a way that won't annoy you." You are trying to get your teenager to see that you are willing to be reasonable if he or she will try to solve the problems concerning certain untidy habits.

THIRD STEP

Some teenagers will come up with very reasonable terms that you can accept, such as, "I'll pick up all of my things at the end of each day before I go to bed," or, "I'll take all my things out of the living room before dinner."

If you are presented with an idea that feels acceptable, say, "That sounds reasonable. Let's try it for a couple of weeks and see how it works." If it works well, you can just continue in the same way, remembering to thank your teenager periodically for cooperating.

FOURTH STEP

If you have a teenager who refuses to cooperate, say, "Since you can't remember to pick up your things around the house, I will do the organizing for you. Right after dinner, I want you to pick up all of your belongings. I will be glad to remind you, but if that doesn't help, I am going to walk around the house with you to see that it gets done. I'll be friendly about it because my purpose is just to get you to pick your things up, and I'll only walk around with you if it's necessary."

If your teenager protests that you treat him or her like a little kid, don't say, "That's right, because you act like one!" Instead say, "I realize that it feels that way, but I guess you'll just have to put up with it until you learn to do it on your own." It is important to say this in a supportive way. Using a nagging or mocking tone will only cause resistance and make it more difficult for both of you.

When you take control in this way, you show your teenager that you know what you want of him or her and that you intend to follow through each time. Eventually, the unpleasant feeling that you are intruding by supervising this task will prompt the kid to pick up belongings on his or her own. When you are supportive and firm, your teenager will find out it's less annoying to get the task done independently.

GETTING ALONG WITH OTHERS

Relatives

Around the age of fourteen or fifteen, the same kid who used to love spending time with grandparents, cousins, or other family members suddenly decides that relatives are a bore. This teenager may claim to be a foundling who couldn't possibly be related to any of these people—they are too weird! This attitude drives parents up the wall and often hurts their feelings.

It is normal for teenagers to resist spending much time with their relatives, complaining about having to call their grandparents or go with the family to visit them. Their chief complaints about socializing with relatives are that there is nothing to do at their grandparents', their cousins are boring and don't know what's happening, and they would rather just be with their friends.

Parents usually feel that the teenager has become selfish and disrespectful. This usually leads to conversations like the following: The parent opens with, "Someday you'll be sorry for your attitude toward your grandparents. You know, they're not going to live forever. You really hurt their feelings when you say you don't want to be with them, especially since they've done so much for you."

The teenager scrambles to come up with a reasonable defense. "You know I love Grandma and Grandpa. It's just that I don't have enough time to see my friends." The outraged parent replies, "Don't give me that! You're always hanging out with your friends."

"Well, it's just that all Grandma talks about is how cute I was when I was a baby. Or they ask me about school." The parent replies, "You're so self-centered. Can't you ever think about someone else for a change? Grandma is really interested in what you're doing." This kind of exchange usually ends with grumbles and only increases the teenager's resistance to the parent's request.

The parent's agenda is for the teenager to show respect and consideration for their relatives and help maintain that important sense of family. Some parents worry about what their relatives will think of their teenager's poor attitude. They don't want to hear complaints or criticism about their kids. Their discomfort leads them to pressure their teenager into socializing with relatives, but the results are frequently unsatisfactory.

The teenagers' agenda in this case relates to the developmental task of learning to separate from their parents. Although they may appear to be selfish, inconsiderate kids, they are actually struggling to lead their own lives, distinct from those of their parents and relatives. They are beginning to make choices about how they want to spend their time. This is a necessary step in growing into adulthood. Unfortunately, at times this agenda will take the form of inconsiderate behavior.

Some parents reading this may be thinking, So, does this guy just expect me to accept that my kid is growing up and ignore his [her] attitude? No, I don't expect that, but I will try to give you some more effective ways to influence your teenager's attitude toward socializing with relatives.

FIRST STEP

Say to your teenager, "You know, I was thinking about our arguments about going to visit your grandparents. Sometimes I've asked you to go when you really don't want to. I should have explained to you why this is important to me without making you feel that you are selfish or unfair to your grandparents. I'm sorry for that. I really didn't want to make you feel guilty about this."

SECOND STEP

Say, "I understand that if I were your age, I might find it boring to visit my relatives. I know that now that you are not a little kid anymore, it's not that much fun to spend your free time with relatives."

THIRD STEP

Tell your teenager, "I really want to hear how you feel about visiting your grandparents because I think it's important that I try to understand your feelings about this." Be prepared to listen nonjudgmentally, without objecting, contradicting, or defending your relatives.

FOURTH STEP

Explain to your teenager, "You are so important to your grandparents. I can see how happy they are when you're with them, and that is important to me. I know you are one of the most meaningful people in their lives. So I would really appreciate it if we could agree on the times when you will be willing to see and call them. I really want you to tell me what seems fair to you."

The procedures in this section apply to all situations involving relatives and close friends. By demonstrating that you understand why your teenager has little interest in the relatives, you reduce his or her resistance to understanding your point of view. When your teenager realizes that his or her feelings are being considered, a reasonable way to meet their needs and yours can usually be negotiated.

You need to remind yourself continually that this behavior is a normal part of growing up and not just the behavior of a selfish, inconsiderate snot. Nor is it evidence of your failure as a parent.

Family Events

Family events or activities are supposed to promote a spirit of togetherness and enjoyment. This occurs in many families when the children are young, but when the kids become teenagers they are simply not as interested in birthday parties, picnics, and holidays with the family. Parents feel mildly disappointed but plunge ahead, encouraging their teenagers and trying to convince them that they really will have a great time. The effort usually results in less than a total success.

As teenagers begin to evaluate with whom and in what way they want to socialize, their choices may not include many family events. The parent's fantasy would be that the teenager would say, "Gee, Mom and Dad, would you like me to go because it's important to you?" I'm sorry, but that's asking your teenager for much too much maturity. The teenage agenda is to keep making life choices that may not satisfy anyone but him- or herself.

Parents want teenagers to feel the same way about being with the family as they did in the past. That is understandable but not very likely. As difficult as it may seem at times, it is important that parents understand their teenager's changing needs. Let's see if we can help your teenager feel understood, while also making clear your needs in this situation.

FIRST STEP

Be observant. Think about how you want your teenager to participate in family events, and be realistic about what you can expect, keeping in mind that his or her social needs have changed. You will need to work together on this issue calmly, before you're invited to Aunt Wilma's annual barbecue. Don't just react angrily at the time of the event, and then forget the issue until the next time the family is getting together.

SECOND STEP

Tell your teenager, "I was thinking about how I felt about family events when I was your age. I began to dread some of the activities that I really loved when I was younger. Do you feel that way sometimes?" If the reply is no, stop reading this section. Most teenagers will say yes, so then you can say that you really understand those feelings because you have felt the same way. Make it clear that you accept such feelings as normal.

THIRD STEP

Tell your teenager, "The next time I get upset at you about this issue, remind me that we had this conversation and that I promised to try to be understanding. But I really would like it if we could agree on some events that you will still attend. I miss the fun we had when you were younger."

FOURTH STEP

If you have a teenager who is very uncooperative after you show this type of understanding, say, "I am going to let you know which family events are really important to me, and I will ask you to be there even if you don't want to go. There are a few that I will just say you have to attend, and I understand that you won't be happy about this. But it won't happen all the time."

Try to give your teenager as much autonomy as possible, but if you don't get cooperation, you have a right to be firm and in control. Don't resort to saying, "You're a selfish brat," even if you feel like it. Remember not to make a big issue over this attitude because you will just increase the kid's resistance to wanting to share time with the family.

Siblings

As siblings get older, they either begin to develop better relationships with each other or they continue to be competitors and rivals. Most teenagers argue a good deal with their siblings, this behavior is very normal throughout adolescence. Teens begin to complain to their parents about siblings, saying, "Mom, he's such a pain! Can't you stop him from being so obnoxious? He's such a brat, and you never discipline him." Underneath their complaints, you may sense the message, "You brought him into the world. I never asked for a brother. *Do* something!"

Sometimes siblings seem to take pleasure in irritating or provoking each other. "Stay out of my room and keep your hands off my clothes." "Your friends are really weird." "Where'd you get such an ugly boyfriend?" "Dad, I'm going to kill her if she doesn't shut up!"

After listening to weeks of endless bickering and baiting, parents may decide that their offspring are horrendous and should be confined to a monastery for life.

Unobservant parents react like this: "You kids are impossible when you're together!" In the same vein, the best-known but least effective comments include, "You're going to be sorry if you don't become friends. You only have one brother [sister]. If you don't start being friends now, it will be too late!"

This usually sends the teenager into fits of derisive laughter, with the siblings joining in. For a moment they are in agreement.

It is normal for siblings to have mixed feelings about each other as they progress through adolescence. Sarcasm, criticism, and bickering are normal ways for many teenagers to relate to one another, but they will develop more positive ways as they get older. In fact, these noisy interactions have a positive value because they allow siblings to work out their feelings of anger and ambivalence toward each other. The same siblings who treat each other harshly in their youth can grow up to be very close friends. Nonetheless, parents need methods for helping siblings learn better behavior toward one another, if only to relieve the noise level in the house.

FIRST STEP

You need to ask yourself this tough question: Do you model behavior that teaches your children how people should get along with others? What kind of example do you set? Do you argue a great deal with your children and your spouse? If the answer is yes, you can't ask your teenager to exercise better control than you do.

If your own interactions need to improve, tell your teenager, "Look, we are asking you guys to work on your arguing, and your dad and I are going to try to stop our arguing, too."

SECOND STEP

Tell your teenager, "I would like to see if you two can try to get along better. I don't want to keep reacting to your fights, and it makes me sad that you are so unfriendly toward each other. We would all be happier if you could get along. Do you have any ideas for improving the situation?"

Begin by asking them to just listen to each other. Let them express their complaints about each other without interrupting or defending either of them. Then ask, "How do you think we can improve these difficulties?"

THIRD STEP

If they can come up with some good suggestions, praise them for their reasonable ideas. Then say, "We'll try this for a week and then talk again. Let's see if talking will help you control your arguing."

FOURTH STEP

If the arguing doesn't decrease after negotiating, say, "The arguing has to stop. I tried hard to let you solve this problem, but since you haven't, I am going to make the rules about this issue. I don't really want to treat you like little kids, but I will if I have to.

"From now on, if you don't stop arguing when I ask you, I will ask you once more. If you don't stop after my second reminder, the one who keeps arguing will face a consequence." Consequences may include not going out on Saturday, not using the phone for the rest of the week, and so on. The key to using consequences successfully is to think of one that is meaningful to your kids and to tell them in advance what it will be.

FIFTH STEP

When siblings are not getting along most of the time, it is helpful to remember that most siblings really care about each other. Therefore, no matter how much you focus on their unacceptable behavior, it is essential to let them know in a noncritical way how important you feel their relationship to one another is.

This is a very important parental statement: "I love you both so much that it makes me feel sad when you don't get along. I know you're going to argue sometimes, but I hope you will also remember that you really care about each other. I can tell that both of you have a difficult time saying that you are sorry. It's not easy, even for adults. Just try to remember that you love each other, even if you argue."

SIXTH STEP

If you have teenagers who don't seem to like each other, it is important to tell them, "I wish I could find some way to help you like each other more, but I know I can't do that. It will really be sad if you don't discover what wonderful qualities both of you possess."

As a parent, you need to be more observant of your reaction to sibling interaction. Take time to state clearly that the reason you are setting consequences for arguing is that you feel strongly that siblings need to learn to love each other and interact in a more positive way.

Although I believe that much of this rivalry is normal behavior and eventually subsides, parents can have a great positive influence on siblings' attitudes toward one another.

Adult Company in the Home

When you had company in your home a few years ago, your kids were excited and happy to meet Mom and Dad's friends or boss. But something begins to change in the teenage years. The same kid who was fascinated by your friends is now totally uninterested, disappears into his room, or asks if she can go out with her friends. You're really lucky if you have a teenager who still enjoys you and your friends.

You probably have mixed feelings about this. Sometimes it's more relaxing for you to entertain without having the kids around. Other times you want your kids to socialize and be a part of things. But many teenagers feel uninterested, uncomfortable, and even embarrassed when they are forced to socialize with adult friends of the family.

By now you have probably gathered that the teenage agenda is to be less and less a part of your world. Socializing with family friends feels like something little kids do. Unfortunately, this feeling of immaturity is reinforced by adults who ask boring, patronizing questions, appear to be uncomfortable talking to teenagers, or talk as if the teenager is still six years old.

When forced to socialize, teenagers often respond in ways that drive their parents crazy. They mumble or grumble and hope that adults will stop asking questions like, "How's school? Did you have a good summer?" Or worse, "Do you have a girlfriend yet?" At this point most teenagers can no longer hide their discomfort, so they roll their eyes, shrug, and say no and then head for the nearest exit.

Parents watching and listening to exchanges like this wonder why their kid is such a social dud. All parents hope that their children will be well-adjusted, socially-aware young adults, reflecting the years of hard work it took to raise them. How easily that fantasy is ruined!

Typically, after an unspectacular social appearance, parents will say to their teenager, "Why do you act like you can't talk when my friends come over? You never shut up around your friends. And the way you answer them is so rude. I was really embarrassed." Your teenager is ready for this. "What do you want me to say? They ask the same dumb questions every time they see me!" The kid feels criticized by your remarks, resorts to grumbling, and walks away again.

Parents don't usually intend to hurt their teenagers' feelings with those remarks. They may be acting out of frustration because such behavior makes them wonder if he or she will ever be an outgoing, friendly adult. Or they may feel that this lack of social skills reflects badly on them. Some relative or friend may make them feel that through remarks or criticism. In any case, parental anxiety and negative remarks only increase a teenager's resistance to change.

If you are very observant, you may have noticed that your teenager likes to talk to some of your friends and may even hang around long after you expected him or her to disappear. No explanation may even be forthcoming, but the key is probably in the way the adult is relating.

If you watch, you will probably see a certain style and content to the conversation. Instead of asking superficial questions, the adult will discuss topics that are interesting to teenagers, such as music, sports, and films. Some teenagers can be very engaging conversationalists if they are given the proper opening, and they respond well when they are treated with interest and respect.

Let's see if we can create a better understanding between you and your teenager about company in the home.

FIRST STEP

You must learn to accept that most of the time your teenager's reluctance to socialize is just part of growing away from you, and the grumbling will disappear with maturity. At this age the adult world and the teen world seem miles apart, but this will change. It may help to repeat to yourself, "This is just a phase. It will pass."

SECOND STEP

Show your teenager that you understand why he or she behaves this way. Say, "I want you to know that I understand and accept the fact that you might be bored or uncomfortable talking to our friends when they come over. I'm sorry that they ask you the same questions that you can't stand hearing from me. But it's only because they don't know what else to say. Adults don't always remember what it's like to be your age."

THIRD STEP

Tell your teenager, "I really want my friends to see what a great kid you are, but I guess that's my problem, not yours." This conveys that you know that sometimes your expectations are not fair. "Can we discuss what would be comfortable for you when we do have company?"

FOURTH STEP

Be clear about your expectations. Say, "I don't expect you to be around most of the time when we have company. But I would appreciate it if you could find some way to be a little friendlier when people come over. Maybe you could answer their questions with a little more information, that's all. For example, when Mrs. Larsen asks you about school, maybe you could say, 'I'm having a good year' or 'I'm doing well in most of my classes but I really have to work on chemistry.' If you could do that much, I really would appreciate it."

Tell your teenager you will try to remind him or her of this conversation in a positive way, without being critical or nagging.

TEENAGERS' NEED FOR PRIVACY

A continuing theme in the teenager's struggle to become an adult is the need for privacy. Having some privacy, a place to be unobserved and unsupervised, gives teenagers a sense of independence and the feeling of having their own lives.

Another reason for the intense need for privacy is the teenager's need to spend time thinking about romantic and sexual feelings. As teenagers become more aware of themselves as sexual and romantic beings, they feel shy or even guilty. They feel that it would be embarrassing for their parents to know their romantic thoughts and feelings. Because they are not yet comfortable with their own sexuality, teenagers are often very self-conscious about letting their parents know about many of their feelings.

For example, when your teenager is with his girlfriend, he doesn't want anyone to hear the intimate way that he is talking or notice the affectionate way that he behaves. This relationship also feels very special and grown-up. Being totally separate from the parents allows him to imagine that he is really an adult, not someone's kid.

These natural developmental stages create an intense desire for separateness. Many teenagers experience great frustration because they feel that they have little privacy at a time when they think they deserve the privacy and consideration given to an adult. As they mature and become more comfortable with themselves, the need for privacy diminishes.

For the parent involved, it is hard not to feel rejected by the teenager's demands for privacy. Just when the kid is getting to be a really interesting person, he or she doesn't even want to be in the same room as you! And unfortunately, the message is often delivered in a harsh manner as the kid throws you a snotty look, yells at you to stay out of his or her room, and then slams the door.

As a parent you may be very confused by this behavior. Is something wrong with your teenager? Is he or she depressed or in trouble? Another problem occurs because your teenager's behavior may also arouse the feeling that you're not needed anymore, and that can be very painful.

Although this may be difficult, it will help you to see this behavior as a struggle for autonomy rather than a personal rejection. You need to show a great deal of understanding for your teenager's need for privacy. In the following section, I will discuss how teenagers use their private time and what it means to them.

Your Teenager's Room

At a certain age, except when asleep or seriously ill, you can't keep your child in his or her room. When adolescence sets in, the child who was very social and wanted to be with other people all the time—who was always underfoot, asking questions, wanting to help you or just hang around—suddenly disappears. Your teenager can't be budged out of his or her room with dynamite!

What goes on in that room all the time? Your curiosity may be so aroused that you fantasize about drilling holes in the walls to see what's going on. (The kid certainly won't tell you!) Is your teenager daydreaming, writing the great American novel, or doing some of those unmentionable things that parents dread?

Sometimes you don't need a peephole to find out. With the stereo at near-criminal volume, your teenager's eardrums are being blown out and his or her brains scrambled. What's worse is that the kid's philosophy of life seems to be developing from the lyrics of the hottest new album. It's enough to drive you crazy!

The teenager's view is that that room is the only place where he or she can feel in total control of life. That explains such phrases as,

"It's my room. Don't touch my things. You have no right to go through my things. You can't just walk in anytime. It's my room!"

The in-room agenda is to hide from the world, have some privacy, and zone out. Zoning out, which consists of traveling through the cosmos without ever leaving the room, is usually accompanied by a strange look in the eyes or a blank stare.

Parents have various concerns about the amount of time that teenagers spend in their rooms. Some parents feel anxious simply because they don't know what the kid is doing for so long. Is he or she just wasting valuable time? Something wrong must be going on or the door wouldn't be closed. Maybe I should just break in and catch him or her in the act!

Other issues that arise for parents of hibernating teenagers are: how long (and how loud) should he or she play music or talk on the phone, and how much privacy with girl- or boyfriend is safe?

Some parents begin to worry about their child's emotional health. They think that the voluntary isolation is a sign of depression and wonder if they should call the family doctor or a therapist. In most cases, it's just typical teenage behavior.

Other parents feel cut off and rejected because their teenager clearly prefers being alone to being with them. But some just feel relief because at least that way they aren't arguing so much. If you are having lots of problems with your teenager, you may want to encourage this need for seclusion just to give yourself a break.

You may feel all these things from time to time, but just try to remember that the need for privacy is a normal developmental phase that will pass, and you will see your child again. Meanwhile, let's see if we can make this issue more manageable for parents and teenagers.

FIRST STEP

If your teenager is functioning well but likes to spend time in his or her room, it's normal. Don't say, "Do you have to live in that room? Get out here!" Being critical only increases the desire to stay in the room and avoid you.

If your teenager is having difficulty functioning and stays in his or her room a lot, it probably suggests some problems. If this is so, you can say, "I wonder if things haven't been going very well lately because you seem to be in your room so much more. I am only saying this because I am concerned. I really care about you, and I hope you will try to talk about it if something is bothering you. I'm not saying this to intrude. I'm just asking because I don't want you to feel alone."

If you get no response, don't push it. Try again later or at another time. This lets the teenager know that you care.

SECOND STEP

If your teenager is generally functioning well and stays in his or her room to study, watch TV, or just be alone, say, "I want you to know that I understand that there are times when you need to be alone in your room. Sometimes I yell at you for being in your room, but usually I'm just upset because of the things that you haven't done. I'm really not criticizing you for staying in your room so much. But there are a few issues that we need to straighten out." In this way you show that you respect your teenager's need for privacy.

THIRD STEP

Since many teenagers get upset if they are bothered when they are in their rooms, you will need to negotiate a reasonable way to intervene. Tell your teenager that there are a few things that you need considered. "Sometimes I need you to come out of your room because I need you to do something. How can I accomplish that without annoying you?"

Ask for suggestions and really try to listen to them. For example, your teenager may suggest that you just knock on the door but not yell that he or she come out. Don't say, "I yell because you never listen." Be a good observer and admit that sometimes your behavior may be inappropriate. Agree that you will try not to yell if he will try to respond sooner to your request. "If you are more cooperative when I call you out of your room, I will try to be more patient when you say that you'll be out in a few minutes."

FOURTH STEP

If your teenager has a television or stereo in his or her room, say that you want to clarify some rules concerning their use. "I know that you like to watch TV and listen to music a lot, and as long as you act responsibly concerning your homework, grades, and your chores, I'm going to leave the amount of time that you watch TV or listen to music up to you." Be realistic. As long as the kid is functioning well, he or she should be able to decide about how to use spare time.

If you are a parent who has strong feelings about your kids watching excessive amounts of television, just limit it, but do it with some understanding of your teenager's feelings. For example, you might say, "I know this doesn't seem fair but I feel very strongly that watching too much television isn't good for you. I realize that you won't agree, but that's my rule. It has nothing to do with how well you behave or perform in school. It's just something that I believe. It's okay if you don't agree." Don't get defensive if your teenager reacts negatively, and don't argue about the issue. Just understand that television is difficult to give up.

SIXTH STEP

Concerning both music and television, if your teenager doesn't respond to the negotiations, remember to simply say that you will limit the amount of time for these activities if you get no cooperation with your requests. These are negotiable issues if the rules are followed.

Remember what we said about consequences. Don't overreact and say, "No music for a month!" You encourage positive behavior with small daily issues when your consequences allow your teenager to follow your rules and regain control of things that are important to him or her.

Teenagers in Their Rooms with Boy- or Girlfriends

One of the smaller issues that causes great concern for many parents is the combination of their teenager, the boyfriend or girlfriend, and the bedroom door—to close or not to close! When parents watch their teenager disappear in the bedroom with someone special in tow and close the door, both the danger flag and their blood pressure go up. Parents who tend to get a little nuts about this issue are relieved if their kid doesn't even know anyone of the opposite sex. Terrified parents want to announce, "I take it all back about asking you to develop social skills. You can be as socially retarded as you want about this issue. Take your time! Twenty-five or thirty is soon enough!"

Some parents just avoid this thorny issue by simply making a rule that teenagers can't be in the room alone with boyfriends or girlfriends, at all, ever. No exceptions! So then the parents' problem is solved, but the teenagers feel that they're being treated unfairly or that they're just not trusted.

Parents have a variety of concerns about unsupervised activities in the bedroom. Some fear that the teenagers are experimenting with drugs. Others are afraid that the privacy of the bedroom is too great a temptation for curious, energetic adolescents who are "in love." Some parents simply believe that it is improper for adolescents of the opposite sex to be alone in a room for extended periods of time.

But most parents' concerns stem from their discomfort about the teenager's awakening sexuality. Even the most liberal parents, who have always felt comfortable with the subject of sex and their own sexuality, still struggle watching their children grow into sexual beings. It is difficult for them to accept that their child now has the needs and desires of an adult, including sex. When sexual needs become more obvious, it forces parents to acknowledge how much their child has grown up.

Parents are also struggling with the issue of values. They want their children to share their values, particularly in the area of sex. And finally, when teenagers begin to behave sexually, to have boy-friends or girlfriends, it creates the awareness that someone else is very significant in their lives, and this is sometimes painful for parents.

If you were able to be direct with your teenager about this issue, you would probably say, "You are not mature enough to control your impulses if you are alone in that room, so keep the door open. It makes me nervous worrying about you."

The teenager's attitude is, "You guys don't trust me. What do you think we're going to do just because the door is closed? We just want some privacy so we can talk and spend time together." If your teenager was able to be direct with you, he or she would say, "Do you really think we are going to have a passionate interlude with you and Dad in the next room?"

Since this tends to be a very emotional topic, let's see if we can clarify some of the issues. First, is it reasonable to think that your teenager would feel comfortable enough to do much of anything sexual with you in the house? Teenagers would probably not feel any more comfortable than adults feel about making love when their own children are up and wandering about the house. Even a closed door doesn't make it feel safe or private enough. If teenagers want privacy for the purpose of sexual experiences, they usually find much better places than their parents' homes.

My experience tells me that whether doors are open or closed, teenagers are not going to put themselves in embarrassing situations over sexual issues. So the desire to go into their rooms and close the door is usually just an expression of the need for privacy for the purpose of learning about relationships and love.

You may be getting the message that closed doors aren't a big issue unless your teenager has been sexually active or irresponsible or you are sure there is a problem. However, I most certainly want to take into account the fact that parents have a variety of values around this issue, all of which will be considered as we discuss handling this problem.

FIRST STEP

Stop hinting to your teenager about what's going on in that room with the boy- or girlfriend, because you both know what you're getting at. Express yourself as clearly as possible.

SECOND STEP

Think about the reason for your discomfort with this issue and why you have made rules. Do you have a teenager whom you have very little reason to mistrust? Is he or she generally responsible? Do you have very little reason to worry about what would go on privately in his or her room with the boy- or girlfriend? Do you believe your teenager just wants to talk?

If you have no reason not to trust your teenager, say, "I realize that when I want you to keep your door open when your boy[girl]friend is over, it makes you feel that I don't trust you. It sounds like I think that you two will have a hard time controlling your sexual attraction."

Some parents are already thinking, This guy is crazy! Am I supposed to come straight out and admit that? Yes, because both you and your teenager know that's what is worrying you. Why else would the door need to be open?

THIRD STEP

When your teenager acknowledges feeling mistrusted, then you should say, "I realize that it doesn't seem fair when you haven't given

80

me any reason to mistrust you. It's just difficult for me to accept how grown-up you are and that you are not my little kid anymore."

FOURTH STEP

Your teenager might appropriately challenge you by saying, "Well, if you admit that you're wrong, why can't I close my door if I feel the need?" If you feel that there is truly nothing to worry about, you should say, "I really have to learn to trust you, so if you want to close your door some of the time when your boy[girl]friend is here, it's okay."

If you do not think it is proper for teenagers to be alone in a closed room, or if you are simply not comfortable with this solution, use this approach. Tell your teenager, "I really do trust you, and I don't believe you're going to do anything wrong in your room. But in my view, it's just not appropriate for you to close the door. I realize that you might not agree and I accept that, but you will have plenty of time when you get older to be alone with your boy[girl]friend." Don't argue this point with your teenager.

If your teenager's sexual behavior has been inappropriate when he or she was in his or her room with his or her girl- or boyfriend, you should consider the approach that follows.

FIRST STEP

Say, "I want to learn to trust you to follow our rules. But you need to show me that you're willing to cooperate. What can we agree upon?" Your teenager may come up with a reasonable suggestion, such as, "If my boy[girl]friend agrees to apologize and we keep the door to my room open, is that acceptable?"

You should say, "As long as you understand that you can't close the door. That is not negotiable. If you are willing to be together with the door open, we will try it and see how it goes."

SECOND STEP

If your teenager says after a while, "Why can't we have the door closed?" don't feel that you have to change your position. You can simply say, "No. I've decided that this is the most comfortable way for me. By keeping the door open, we won't have any mistrust and I won't worry about what you're doing. I realize that might seem unfair but that's my rule."

Remember, you don't always have to agree with your teenager's feelings, and if your teenager has demonstrated some difficulty in controlling sexual impulses, this is extremely fair.

Parties at Home

When your teenager suggests throwing a party in your home, you may want to have some terrific excuses ready. You might say that you had to include a "teenage party clause" when you bought the house: One teenage party and the family will be living in a trailer! Or you could simply move the house off its foundation the night of the party. (They may do that for you anyway.) Of course, the most effective way to avoid having a teenage party is to avoid having a teenager. Too late for that solution!

When your child was small, a party at your house was cute, memorable, even fun. Ice cream, cake, a few games, and you were set until the next year. The worst thing that usually happened was that some kid would eat too much and throw up on the rug. When your teenager suggests a party, you worry that your house, your reputation, and the neighborhood may never be the same!

Why all this terrible talk about teenage parties? How did they get such a bad reputation? Well, perhaps it's because teenagers have been known to leave a party with half the contents of the house in their pockets. Occasionally they trash everything in their path, transforming the yard and surrounding neighborhood into a junkyard. Not to mention the deafening music that seems to be required, even at the tamest teenage gatherings. In short, the teenagers' contribution to society is rarely demonstrated at parties.

Your teenager's agenda in having a party is to develop his or her social standing. Hosting a party increases social acceptance, especially if the party's a big hit. Parties also give teenagers a chance to socialize with particular kids they like without risking personal rejection by asking them out on a date.

The parents' agenda is to allow their teenager this social experience without giving up control of their home. They want their teenager to act responsibly. Those are reasonable expectations, but how do you arrange it?

FIRST STEP

If your teenager asks about having a party, you should say, "Tell me what you have planned for the party." Then listen to see if he or she has thought about any of your concerns. You will want to know how many kids will be at the party. Is it an open party or by invitation only? How will things be kept under control? How will the guests know the rules of the house?

Though it is unlikely that your teenager will have thought these issues through to your satisfaction, the discussion will be a great start. If your teenager has not considered any of your concerns, move on to the second step.

SECOND STEP

Tell your teenager, "Let me tell you what I need you to do in order to have a party at our house. First, I want you to get three or four of your friends who will be responsible for the party with you. I think it's too hard to handle a party by yourself. I want to meet with them once to discuss my expectations about the party. Then I want a list of all the kids coming to the party, with phone numbers."

THIRD STEP

Clearly explain your rules about liquor, drugs, and coming and going during the party. It's not enough to say, "I don't want things to get out of hand!" If someone comes to the party drunk, insist that someone call the parents or arrange for him or her to be driven home.

FOURTH STEP

Define your role as chaperone. It is my opinion that parents must take a very active but not intrusive role in the party. Your teenager may say, "Can't you just stay in another room while we're having the party? You'll embarrass me if you're hanging around."

As a parent, you may be feeling, After all I've done for this kid, it's really some nerve to call me an embarrassment! What a brat! That is a perfectly normal reaction. However, say, "I understand that it might make you uncomfortable, but that's one of the rules you'll have to accept if you want to have a party here. I'll try not to embarrass you, but I will be in and out of the party to see that your friends are following the rules."

FIFTH STEP

Tell your teenager, "A party is a lot of work and it can be a lot of fun. I really want you to have a great time. If you take care of your part of the agreement, I will be able to let you handle most of the issues at the party. If I see that you and your friends are handling things well, I'll stay out of your way."

SIXTH STEP

If your teenager's friends don't respect authority or the people giving the party, don't let your teenager talk you into trying another party. If you never let them have a single party at your house, it won't ruin their development or their social life! There's nothing in the parent's manual that says to be a good parent you must let your teenager have a party.

3

BEHAVIOR OUTSIDE THE HOME

"There's a monster in the streets!"

Curfew

Curfew refers to any time that you ask your teenager to be home at a certain time, not just when he or she is out with friends at night. Curfew includes coming home after school, being home during the day, or coming home by a specific time in the evening. Understandably, parents are more concerned about evening hours, but it is important to establish clear communication about any expectations or concerns that you have in this area.

A typical parent-teenager dialogue about curfew goes something like this: "I told you to be home at ten-thirty. Where were you? You're so irresponsible!" The teenager replies, "I couldn't get home on time because my ride didn't come." In no mood for excuses, especially old ones, the parent says, "Well, you'll just have to plan better." The teenager is now feeling criticized and defensive. "You always blame me, even when it's not my fault." The rare teen will just blurt out the truth, "I lost track of time!" The dialogue is complete when the parent screams, "I'm sick of your excuses," and the teenager returns the sentiment with a dirty look.

Curfew is an important issue for parents because it helps them deal with the concerns and fears that come from having a teenager who is out in the world. Suddenly the kid is gone for hours after dark, and your imagination can go wild. Is she safe? Is he a good driver? Can they be trusted?

All this speculating can drive parents a little nuts. Some parents can't sleep until their kids are safely home. They walk the floor, look out the window five hundred times, and eventually begin talking to themselves until the kid gets home. When the kid finally sails in, it's to be blown out the door by the frantic question, "Where have you been?" Although the parent's distress is obvious, the teenager rarely understands that the anger is actually a sign of concern or worry.

Most teenagers' attitude about curfew is that they are too old and mature to require restrictions. To them it's just another version of bedtime. They're rarely in agreement with their parents' ideas about curfew and are constantly offering examples of the more lenient curfews their friends enjoy. A major complaint is that they're being treated like infants.

Parents feel that when their teenager doesn't follow rules about curfew, the kid is potentially out of control and is flaunting disdain for their authority. But the average teenager is doing neither. He or she is just having a good time with friends, and it's very difficult to stop doing it just to be home on time.

If adults had curfews, they'd have the same problems. Just think about your spouse or some of your relatives who are otherwise very responsible but have difficulty being on time and frequently lose track of time, especially when they are doing something they enjoy. You might have even done this once or twice yourself. Parents who are poor observers of their own behavior may not have noticed that they have the same difficulties with punctuality as their kids

FIRST STEP

You need to think about how clearly you have dealt with the issue of your teenager's schedules and curfews. Have you made or discussed specific rules about curfew or do you just get upset after the fact? Are you inconsistent in enforcing the rules that you have established? Are your expectations vastly different from those of most parents?

SECOND STEP

Remember that your teenager will probably tell you that other parents are more liberal than you about curfews. You will hear complaints such as, "Sean doesn't even have a curfew on weekends." "Jenny gets to stay out until one and you make me come home by eleven. It's so embarrassing!" Objections about daytime curfews may include, "Why can't I go to the mall after school and stay until five? All the other kids do!"

Don't get defensive or respond in an irritated tone with remarks such as, "I don't care what the other kids get to do. You're going to do what I say!" Instead, I hope you will consider this approach. Say, "I can understand that you want to stay with your friends when you're having a good time. I realize that you wish I was more like the other parents, but I have different rules about curfew. The difficult thing about being a kid is that you have to follow rules that you don't like, and this is one of them. When you're older you won't have any of these rules, and I understand that you can't wait for that day." In this way you show great understanding for the teenager's point of view but you don't change your rules.

THIRD STEP

Try to remember your own experience of having to obey a curfew when you were a teenager. Take a few minutes with your teenager to share your recollections. Don't do this on the run or when you have other issues to discuss. Say, "I was thinking about what it was like when I was a teenager and my dad would give me a curfew. I didn't like it either. I realize that most of the time when you get home late, it's not because you don't want to follow the rules. It's just that it's difficult to leave your friends when you are enjoying yourself. I really understand that you just want to have fun, and the rules seem dumb at the moment. However, you still have to learn to be on time, so I've come up with a new idea."

FOURTH STEP

Tell your teenager, "I realize that it's not always easy to be on time, so I have decided that you can have a half-hour grace period when you are out in the evening at a concert, party, or movie. I will give you a fifteen-minute grace period for daytime schedules. If you can arrive within that time, we will have no problem."

Some parents would say, "This guy is crazy! Why should I reward my kid when he [she] can't or won't follow the rules?" Well, I know that if your teenager feels fairly treated, he or she is likely to be more motivated to improve his or her behavior. Establishing a grace period is a way of saying that you feel that the kid's life is important, too.

FIFTH STEP

If your teenager continues to ignore curfews, even with your efforts to negotiate, it's time to say the following: "I have tried to be as understanding as I know how to be. But this hasn't helped you learn to be more responsible about getting home on time. So from now on if you ignore your curfew, this will be the rule. Each time you are more than ten minutes late [be realistic and give a bit of leeway] you will stay home the next weekend." Use this or any other appropriate consequence we have discussed. Tell your teenager that the consequences will be increased each time this behavior occurs, until you get more cooperation. Remember that if your teenager improves after three weeks or less, you can renegotiate your arrangement.

However, with a teenager who has a pattern of irresponsibility, don't keep renegotiating. This situation just needs very firm limits. Remember, when you begin to see a positive change in behavior, even if it is very small, let the kid know that you appreciate the effort.

Staying Overnight with Friends

When your teenager was younger, you were probably pleased when she was invited to sleep over with friends. It meant that she was popular and you didn't have to worry about her ability to socialize and make friends. It also meant that you had a child-free evening without having to hire a baby-sitter. Now that she is a teenager, you don't usually worry about whether she is socializing, but rather what she is doing when she is socializing.

At some time or another, most teenagers will test the limits of parental authority. This is a very normal impulse for teenagers—not the first step to delinquency! It's rather exciting to outmaneuver a parent in order to get your own way, and one of the best times to try this maneuver is when staying overnight with friends.

Parents know this and they respond with misgivings and questions. When their teenager asks if she can stay overnight with a friend, parents immediately brush up on their FBI skills. What is she really going to do? Some parents only resist with difficulty the urge to follow their kids and stake out the neighborhood with high-powered binoculars, collecting evidence to confirm their suspicions and fears.

Maybe you have caught your teenager in a few small lies, and so your suspicions are well founded. Teenagers sometimes omit details that might upset you and cause you to veto their plans—such as the teen who says she's just going over to Jane's house. They're going to stay in and talk. The minor details that drive parents crazy are the fact that the boyfriends are also scheduled to come over, and Jane's parents will be out for the evening. No wonder parents are uneasy about sleepovers.

Teenagers don't really think they are doing anything wrong if they sneak out with a friend and go to a club that you say is off-limits. Their view is that you don't understand and all the other parents let their kids go, so you're just being unreasonable. Unless you are willing to hire a detective or spend your evenings spying on your kid, you will need to work out another way to be comfortable when your teenager spends the night at a friend's house.

FIRST STEP

Ask yourself how you feel about your teenager's friends. How well do you know their parents? Are they very reliable people who would be responsible when your teenager is staying over?

SECOND STEP

If you don't know the answers to these questions, you should take this position. Call the parent of the friend with whom your teenager will be staying. Discuss any concerns or restrictions that you want to be observed. This sends a message to your teenager that you will be involved in her behavior, even when the friend's parents are not at home. It's not that you mistrust her, but it's your way of feeling at ease. Don't let her talk you out of doing this with remarks such as, "God, that will embarrass me! You just don't understand!"

THIRD STEP

Ask your teenager what her plans are for the overnight stay and see if they are acceptable to you. If they're not acceptable, negotiate a compromise between your expectations and hers.

FOURTH STEP

Since even a phone call can't really tell you how responsible any parent will be, tell your teenager that she will be responsible for following your rules, even if the parents don't enforce them, and even if they encourage behavior that you do not allow.

Your rules should be the following: If plans for the evening change at the last minute, your teenager must call and get permission for the new agenda. If she can't reach you by phone, she will have to forgo any activities that have not been approved by you. If she doesn't follow the rules, she won't be allowed to stay over with friends for a specific period of time.

FIFTH STEP

Tell your teenager, "I realize that you probably can get away with things when you are out with your friends. I know that kids your age frequently try to get around their parents. It can be very tempting to say you're doing one thing and then go off and do something else that you know I wouldn't approve. I'm telling you this because I really understand that sometimes you want to do things whether I like it or not. And it seems worth the risk because you're likely to get away with it. I hope you don't test this, because if I find out, I'll have to limit your time with your friends."

In this way you let your teenager know that you understand how she feels. You acknowledge that it's natural to try to get away with things, without condoning or condemning this behavior. Sometimes, when a parent is matter-of-fact about teenage behavior and demonstrates an awareness of the teenager's impulses and dilemmas, the teenager may conclude that it's just not worth it to break the rules.

Teenagers Behind the Wheel

All parents live in fear of the day when their teenager can legally get behind the wheel of a car. Perhaps some of you remember a horror movie called *The Car*, in which a car cruised around the city without a driver, terrorizing neighborhoods and causing mayhem. That's the feeling many parents have on the day their teen gets a learner's permit, and these feelings reach flood level the first time he or she drives off into the sunset—alone!

We can only look back with envy to the days when parents simply had to teach children how to sit on a horse. At least the horse could make some of the decisions! In a car, it's all up to the kid. Insult is added to anxiety when you are forced to meet the insurance agent who quotes phenomenal rates to insure this automotive menace.

All of these issues prompt parents to delay the driving debut as long as possible. When their teenager starts asking about driving, getting a license, or buying a car, parents say things like, "We'll see. We'll talk about it. Not yet." This stalling leads your teenager into an obsessional thought process. His overwhelming concern is getting into that car.

When you avoid this issue, your teenager begins to have a nervous breakdown. The symptoms are grabbing the steering wheel while you are driving, talking endlessly of how cool it's going to be when he can drive, and how his life will be ruined if you won't let him learn to drive. In desperation, he may promise to change his ways (all of them) if only you will get him a car or let him drive!

Since many teenagers behave much better when they are finally given permission to drive, you may be tempted to give yours an unlimited supply of gas and suggest that they drive around continuously until they reach the age of eighteen! This is rarely a practical option, so let's look at some ways to handle this automotive challenge.

FIRST STEP

You need to be very clear about when and under what conditions you are willing to allow your teenager to get a license or drive. Some parents allow teenagers to drive because it is necessary for the family to have another driver. Other parents feel that getting a license is a privilege that is earned through good grades and appropriate behavior, and there are many other conditions. The point is just to be clear about yours.

SECOND STEP

Stop saying things that frustrate your teenager, such as, "We'll talk about your car soon." "I haven't had time to think about it, so just stop bugging me!" Your teenager will never let this issue die because driving a car is just about the most important thing in his life. When you are vague and unclear in your responses, you just increase his obsession.

Avoid saying things like, "After the way you have been behaving this week, how dare you ask me about getting a car?" If getting a car is going to be the consequence for good behavior, you need to set it up in advance.

THIRD STEP

Give your teenager specific guidelines for when he can get his license, practice driving, or get a car. If the criteria for getting to drive are based on improved behavior, define your expectations clearly. If you are using other means to determine when your teenager deserves to get a license or car, be very specific about how you will make your decision.

FOURTH STEP

Once you have decided to bite the bullet and let your teenager drive, have him take as much of the responsibility as possible for making it happen. He can call the DMV, fill out forms, get insurance estimates, and be available when it is convenient for you to proceed.

FIFTH STEP

Be aware of your own level of anxiety when you are driving with your teenager. Stop pointing out all of his driving mistakes because this only makes him irritated with you and decreases his driving skills. Instead, think about saying, "I'll try very hard not to lecture at you about your driving skills if you will try to take my suggestions with a good attitude. This is going to be difficult for both of us to do, but let's make an effort because I really want you to have this opportunity."

Teenage Driving Habits

It is sometimes difficult for parents to understand their teenager's love affair with cars. For an adult, cars mean payments, insurance, unexpected repairs, and endless demands to chauffeur people from place to place. For a teenager, the car is synonymous with freedom. All the autonomy they have been seeking is concentrated behind that wheel.

A car provides access to the world and the mobility to socialize with friends. Finally, its possession is a status symbol.

The teenage boy's agenda when he is driving includes performing antics that will impress his friends and testing his skills, particularly by driving fast, which gives him an intoxicating illusion of control and power. Boys tend to be more impulsive than girls, their judgment is less reliable, and for this reason they tend to collect far more tickets than do girls.

Many girls drive very carefully, apparently because they don't feel the need to impress their peers through feats of skill and daring. But their attention may be diverted from their driving when they are checking out the guys. Boys do this, too.

When teenages get into trouble by collecting a ticket or having an accident, their tendency is to want to hide the incident from their parents. They avoid facing the problem by denying that it exists, eventually creating even greater problems for themselves.

The parent's agenda is to have as much control over this situation as possible without having a complete anxiety attack every time their teenager reaches for the keys. The result is a great deal of stress and worry. Here are some ways that parents might handle the great car wars without incurring permanent damage to their nervous systems.

FIRST STEP

In a calm moment tell your teenager, "Now that you're driving, I need to tell you my concerns. I'm glad that you're so happy to be driving, but I worry about whether you always drive carefully. I really love you and I don't want you to get hurt."

You need to tell him, "I realize that sometimes it will be very tempting to do things like I did when I was your age, such as driving too fast, showing off, and going places that I wouldn't approve. I think these are very natural impulses that we all have sometimes."

If your teenager takes this as criticism or seems to feel that it is unnecessary to listen to you, accept his response and reply calmly. "I'm not saying that you're doing anything wrong, and I understand that you don't feel that you need to hear this. But if you and I can have these discussons occasionally, I think it will be much easier for us to understand each other when a problem comes up." Remember, this is not a twenty-minute lecture. It's a short conversation unless your teenager wants to talk further.

SECOND STEP

Tell your teenager, "If you have an accident or get a ticket and you haven't been acting recklessly, I will try very hard to be understanding. I won't question you as if I know you did something wrong. I know that adults have accidents and get tickets, too. However, if you delay telling me, and I find out from the insurance company or we get a warrant about your ticket, I will restrict your use of the car because of your lack of responsibility. I am telling you this ahead of time so that you will fully understand me and you won't get yourself in this situation."

The observant parent will not react if the teenager doesn't display full understanding or acceptance of the parental position. Don't go on and on once you have made it clear.

THIRD STEP

If a teenager gets tickets or has accidents more than is understandable or acceptable, don't go into lecture number thirty-nine and say, "What's wrong with you? You will never drive as long as you live in this house. I just can't trust you." If your goal is just to make yourself feel better, go ahead and blow off steam! But if it's to create some understanding between you and your teenager, then you need to try to keep your composure. You're probably thinking that's easy for me to say because it's not my kid. I am only saying to do the best that you can, and if you overreact and scream at the kid, come back later and say, "I'm sorry that I overreacted about your ticket, but this issue of cars and driving really worries me. I need you to try harder because your driving is a serious concern for me. I know I'll get used to it as you get older."

FOURTH STEP

If your teenager gets an excessive amount of tickets or is involved in numerous accidents, the courts may have some part in the restriction of his driving, but you need to make your rules extremely clear. Tell him, "If your driving doesn't improve and your problems continue, I will have to take away your driving privileges. It's the last thing I want to do because driving is very important to you and I like to see you happy. But if you can't improve, I will have no choice. I will return your privileges gradually based on your ability to keep your record clean. If you show an accepting attitude toward my position and don't overreact when I have to restrict you, that will show that you are ready to act more responsibly. I really want to work this out with you." In this way you are constantly showing an interest on the teenager's behalf.

FIFTH STEP

If your teenager continues to drive recklessly or drives under the influence of drugs or alcohol, don't treat this as a simple driving problem. It is more likely that the recklessness and disregard are signs of more serious problems, and you need to seek professional help.

Going to Parties

We have already discussed the pleasures and terrors of hosting a teenage party in your home. However, the more common teenage request is to attend a party at another teenager's house. When your teenager is young, between the ages of twelve and fifteen, you may feel less anxiety about letting him or her go to parties because you still provide the transportation, and that gives you a sense of control. It's fairly easy for you to meet the parents who are hosting the party and enforce a curfew. Young teenagers also expect parents to chaperone their parties, so supervision is generally better.

Parents experience much more anxiety when their older teenager heads out the door for a party, driving him- or herself or riding with other teenagers. Curfew violations, reckless driving, and abuse of drugs and alcohol suddenly become real issues, and parents see a long night stretching ahead of them.

They worry about supervision, who's attending, and whether alcohol and drugs will be available. This leads to conversations like "Who's chaperoning? Who's going to be there? If the Coleman kids are invited, you're staying home!"

First the teenager reacts with disbelief and frustration. "How do I know who's going? It's not my party." The tone escalates to sarcasm and criticism. "Sure, Dad, I'll get a list of names and phone numbers for everyone who's invited. God, you're so out of it! Maybe you'd like me to do random drug testing at the door and phone you with the results?"

Every seasoned parent knows the appropriate response to such remarks. "Don't get smart with me or you'll never go to another party as long as you live!" This becomes a loaded issue because parties are very important to your teenager, and your worries are perfectly understandable. Let's talk about another way to handle this issue.

FIRST STEP

When your teenager approaches you about attending a party, you must resist the impulse to ask questions that put the kid on the defensive. Be observant. See if your questions convey an attitude of mistrust or if your tone indicates that the Spanish Inquisition has just been revived. Does it sound as if your real concern is about your teenager's welfare or are you just being difficult and demanding answers?

SECOND STEP

Tell your teenager, "I want to be very clear about what my expectations will be from now on when you ask my permission to go to a party. You'll need to find out who's chaperoning so that I can call that person."

Your teenager may object strenuously. "God, Mom, that's so embarrassing. I'm not a little kid anymore." You need to say, "I understand how you feel, but that's my rule. No discussion. Once in a while, we may not agree about that parties you ask to go to, and I won't be able to let you go. But most of the time I will let you go if you can be responsible."

THIRD STEP

Tell your teenager, "I remember how some kids acted at parties when I was your age, so sometimes I'm concerned about how kids act at your friends' parties. I really need to feel sure that you will use good judgment when you go to parties. I don't want this to sound like a lecture, but I hope you will consider some of these issues.

"If you are at a party and drinking or drugs get out of hand, I really need you to use good judgment and leave. If you have been drinking, I would rather that you call and ask me to bring you home, even if it's late, or get a friend to drive you. Promise me that you won't drive when you've been drinking.

"The last thing I'm going to ask you to do isn't easy. I'm not asking you to squeal on your friends, but if you leave a party because some of the kids are out of control, I would like you to tell me the reason that you left. You might think that if you tell me then the next time I might not let you go, but it would really let me know that you were using good judgment, and I would trust you even more. If you can't do this, it doesn't mean I won't trust you. I will make a real effort to listen to you without getting upset, because I know that's the only way you will learn to confide in me."

Whenever you show your teenagers this kind of respect, they feel understood and are motivated to try to please you. Many of them respond by making a real effort to be more responsible.

FOURTH STEP

If you have a teenager who normally follows rules but continues to go to parties that are not acceptable or doesn't tell you when he or she gets into trouble at parties, then your position has to be tough but fair.

Tell your teenager, "You've gone against the rules too many times, so now I feel that I can't trust you. I hope I will be able to trust you sometime in the future." Despite your firmness, you are still showing your teenager that you have confidence in his or her ability to change. "Because you haven't followed the rules concerning parties, you will be grounded next weekend. That means no visitors and no phone calls.

"When the next party comes up, we'll go over the rules again. If you can follow them, that's terrific. If I find out that you didn't follow the rules, you will be grounded for two weekends, and it will double if it happens after that. Eventually it's not going to be worth it to keep ignoring my rules. I hope you don't cause yourself that kind of problem." Try to deal with the situation in this way—no lectures, no screaming, just fair toughness.

Remember, your teenager may say that it's embarrassing to ask a friend for the name and phone numbers of the parents who will be chaperoning the party. Or they will say that they just can't get that information because they were invited through a friend to an "open" party—one to which anyone is invited. Just say that you understand that it may be a little uncomfortable or difficult, but that's the rule. The responsibility is appropriately put on the teenager. If the kid really wants to go to the party, he or she will have to make that effort. No doubt, your teenager will tell you that the other kids will think it's so uncool! The simplest, least provocative response is, "I'm sorry you feel that way, but that's my rule."

Going to Concerts

Your teenager comes to you and says, "I have to go hear Black Stab" (fictitious name). You demand, "Black *what?* No kid of mine is patronizing a group with a name like that! They're probably perverts or homicidal maniacs. It could be dangerous! What kind of kids go to these concerts?"

"Mom, their album is number one on the charts. They're so hot! All the kids are going! I have to go. I'll just die if I miss this concert!" The urgency that teenagers feel about going to concerts relates to their intense relationship with music and the adventure of going to a musical performance with friends. It's a major social event for many teenagers.

The parents' agenda is to survive the teenager's demands. They worry about drugs, violence, accidents, and the "bad elements" at concerts, collecting newspaper articles about riots and arrests at concerts to strengthen their objections. They're also concerned about who will be going along with their teenager. Even though most parents trust their son or daughter, it is difficult to feel so little control over the situation.

Resist the urge to say, "You're not going to that crazy concert! Don't even ask!" This will send your teenager into orbit, which might be preferable to doing battle about the concert issue. Try to remember that your goal is to have your teenager listen to you with a fraction of the attention he or she gives to a favorite album.

FIRST STEP

It would be very unusual for a teenager to tell you the complete truth about a concert if it would prevent you from granting permission to go. So, if you are worried about the possibility of violence or trouble at a particular concert, you can check with the police to find out if violence has been associated with the performances of a particular group. Do this only if you have heard alarming things about the group.

You can't always rely on your teenager for the truth, because going to the concert may be so important that he or she may deny the reality of any problems. It's not really a deliberate lie but a strong need to believe that what he or she wants to do is safe and reasonable.

SECOND STEP

Tell your teenager, "I really trust you most of the time, but some concerts can get wild so I am a little worried. Tell me how you plan to get to the concert." Allow the kid to think about the responsibility of going to the event without feeling negative pressure from you.

THIRD STEP

Validate any comments from your teenager that suggest mature thinking. For example, if the plan to go with other kids whom you trust and feel are responsible, say, "I'm really glad that you chose Jim and Rick because they seem to use good judgment."

If your teenager hasn't thought it out well, say, "I don't know any of the kids you are going with or how responsible they are. What can we do about that?" He might tell you that they're kids from school, as if that is an adequate recommendation. Tell him, "I need to meet them before you go because I need to tell them my rules about you going to concerts."

Your teenager won't necessarily like this and will probably object. Simply say, "I understand that you don't see why I have to do this, but that's the only way that I can agree to let you go with friends I don't know."

FOURTH STEP

Whether or not you know the friends with whom your teenager will be going to the concert, you should make a point of meeting all the kids and explaining your expectations. "No drugs and no drinking. Also, I want you to come home right after the concert because I know it will be late. If you can do this, you'll be able to do lots of things together. If you don't follow the rules, I'll have to limit your activities together." Say lightly but firmly, "I just want you to know what I expect and I hope you have a great time."

Most teenagers would be surprised if you did this in front of their friends, yet if you can do it in a way that is friendly and understanding, most teenagers will accept it even if they don't like it. It puts positive pressure equally on all of them, not just your kid.

FIFTH STEP

Speak to your teenager alone about the concert. "I really want you to enjoy these events. If you just do the few things that I am asking, I'll try to consider your requests because they will deserve consideration."

If you have a teenager who acts irresponsibly, then say, "Unless you learn to follow the rules, you will not be able to go to many concerts. I'd prefer not to deprive you because I know how important they are to you, but I will if you don't learn that I mean what I say." Unless your teenager's behavior is very antisocial, give several chances to demonstrate your reasonableness and your willingness to have your teenager take control of his or her life.

Parents as Transportation

Prior to the celebrated and dreaded day when your teenager gets that driver's license, you will probably have logged a million miles driving your child and assorted friends or neighbors to school and to soccer, basketball, ballet, Scouts, and the many other after-school activities that occupy children's free time.

In the last thirty years parents have become reluctant to let their children walk, ride bikes, or use buses alone because of the increasing dangers on the streets. As a result, parents spend so much time transporting children that some have resorted to shaving while driving and carrying a change of clothes in the trunk. What did children do before the parent-chauffeur was invented?

Kids in previous generations didn't expect parents to transport them everywhere. They still understood the function of their legs, and their lives were much simpler, whereas contemporary teenagers feel that they are being treated unjustly if they have to walk more than two blocks. Not to mention the indignity of it all. How uncool! Nobody walks or takes the bus to the mall! And the reality is that life *is* more complex, and teenagers have many places that they have to go. That means parents must either surrender the car or become chauffeurs for the teenager's blossoming social life.

Many teenagers develop the habit of asking parents to drive them various places at the last minute, to be on call, and to wait for them or pick up their friends, many times without any warning at all and often without so much as a thank you. The teenagers' attitude is that parents should double as personal chauffeurs until they themselves are able to drive. The usual parental response is to grumble, complain, and lecture the teen but to continue to comply with many of these transportation demands.

This issue of transportation offers an opportunity to teach your teenager a greal deal about responsibility, planning, and learning to be aware of the needs of other people. Because the need for transportation is so important to your teenager and he or she is clearly dependent on your cooperation, there will usually be a strong motivation to develop a sensitivity to your needs in this area. Let's discuss how this can be accomplished.

FIRST STEP

Stop making comments like, "You'd better learn to be more considerate! Don't ask me if I will drive your friends when they are standing right there listening. That really puts me on the spot!" Remarks like that do nothing to clarify what you really expect from your teenager.

SECOND STEP

On this issue you need to consider your own needs carefully. If you're a parent who is always trying to facilitate your teenager's social needs and activities, it's time to evaluate which transportation requests are necessary and legitimate and which are extra. You need to take a good look at what is really convenient for you and what causes excess stress.

THIRD STEP

Your teenager's social needs will generally be positive and healthy, but teens rarely take into account how their need for transportation affects their parents. A parent would go into shock if their teenager said, "Mom, I really appreciate all the driving you do for me and my friends. Is there anything I can do for you? Please tell me if the driving is getting to be too much for you."

Looking at the situation more realistically, even without making excessive demands for transportation, your teenager still needs to learn to be responsible concerning your needs.

Tell your teenager, "I need to tell you some of the feelings that I have when you ask me to drive you and your friends to various places. I'm very happy that you have so many interesting activities and I want you to have fun. But we need to come to a better understanding about what I expect from you when you ask me to drive you or pick you up."

Your teenager may give you the usual innocent remark, "What do you mean?" which really means that he or she is feeling defensive. Say, "I should have told you a long time ago what I expect, so I am not blaming you." Be sure to clarify that the point of the discussion is not to criticize but to avoid problems in the future by talking now.

FOURTH STEP

Tell your teenager, "I don't think you realize how often you wait until the last minute to ask me to drive you somewhere. You seem to think I should always make time to drive you, without even asking about my schedule. I usually say yes, but I also act annoyed and frustrated a lot. I have to work on controlling my frustration, but you have to work on letting me know in advance that you need to be driven somewhere. Once in a while, I don't mind doing things on short notice, but from now on you need to plan better."

FIFTH STEP

Say to your teenager, "From now on, I will tell you what is reasonable for me. Sometimes if your request doesn't work with my schedule, I'll just have to turn you down. I'll tell you it's not convenient.

"Also, from now on I want you to tell me in advance about any of your plans that require transportation. Let's set a time each week to discuss your schedule and mine. You need to think about where you need to be driven during the upcoming week, other than regularly scheduled events."

Planning with your teenager will remove much of the frustration, but there will always be unexpected events. You need to explain your point of view about emergency situations. Say, "Sometimes you tell me that you have a ride arranged and then it doesn't work out, so you call me at the last minute to come and get you and your friends. I don't mind if you have really planned well and something unexpected happens. That isn't your fault." In this way you show that you are willing to be reasonable and flexible.

"But from now on, if you don't plan well or forget to make plans, I won't be available to bail you out unless I see a real improvement in this area. I really need you to realize that I get tired from all the extra driving. I like helping you, but you need to understand that both of us are affected by your transportation needs."

Remember that your tone of voice should be firm but supportive. This is the beginning of teaching your teenager to listen to your needs without feeling your criticism or frustration. Show your appreciation whenever you see consideration. Don't take any efforts for granted.

Calling Home

The battle between parents and teenagers over calling home usually goes something like this: The parent says, "You're trying to tell me that you weren't near a phone all evening, not even for one minute? Someone ought to alert the phone company. They're missing a lot of business in this area!"

The teenager modifies the story slightly. "Well, there were phones, but my friend wouldn't stop."

"Your friend wouldn't stop? That's terrific! Don't give me those lame excuses. I've heard them all a dozen times! Someday you'll call home and the answering machine will announce, 'Family moved. Whereabouts unknown. You're too late!'"

When teenagers don't call home at the appointed time or at all, their parents experience anxiety. They wonder what has happened. Has there been an accident? Is everything all right? Or is this just defiance?

The reason that teenagers frequently neglect to call home is that their agenda when they are out is to become totally involved in their own lives, forgetting that they are attached to a family and parents, ignoring for a time that they are really someone's kid and not a fully grown adult. To keep this illusion going, they make the decision not to call home. They figure that it's worth it to take the punishment afterwards if they can continue to do what they please without interruption or intervention. Many times the punishment is just a few minutes of Mom yelling or being mad, and that's not a bad price to pay for hours of freedom.

Therefore, the parent has to make sure that the teenager who constantly disregards the request to call home discovers that the price is too high to make it worthwhile. Again, with effective discipline you can teach your teenager that being responsible is in his or her best interests. (And, in fairness, you should also keep in mind that adults don't always remember to call home either!)

FIRST STEP

Remember not to go into lecture number 32, "Where were you? Why didn't you call? You do this all the time and I'm sick of it!" Instead, say, "Do you realize that you frequently forget to call home? You probably don't mean to upset me, but I do worry about whether something has happened to you or you have just forgotten to call. I wonder if you can tell me how we can solve this problem?"

Your teenager may start to be defensive, saying things like, "I hardly ever do that!" Just say, "I'm not going to argue about how often it happens, but I want to make sure that it doesn't happen most of the time. Let's see how you do for the next four weeks. We'll keep track and discuss it at the end of each week." When your teenager does call home, be sure to express your appreciation of the effort. Don't just comment about failures.

SECOND STEP

Unless your teenager is extremely irresponsible about phoning in, I don't feel that this issue deserves consequences. It's one of those issues where most teenagers will try harder to be responsible if they receive positive encouragement.

One way to be positive and encouraging, even if your teenager forgets to call, is to say, "I know its not always easy to remember to call, but I really want you to concentrate and remember." If you say this in an understanding way, your teenager is likely to try much harder.

THIRD STEP

When dealing with this issue it will help you to remember that adults also promise to call home, totally forget, and then feel embarrassed or resentful when they are reminded that someone was waiting for their call. Sometimes people, including teenagers, just forget. It's not always a case of defying authority.

Also, being a good observer as a parent means knowing which issues should be dealt with as serious matters and which respond best to a firm, positive attitude. Your attitude, tone of voice, and the feelings you convey greatly influence your teenager's inclination to cooperate or resist.

Hanging Out, Cruising, or Kicking Back

By the time this book goes to press, the terms *hanging out, cruising,* or *kicking back* may have been replaced with other slang terms that describe one of teenagers' favorite pastimes. Whatever the popular phrase, the activity will probably be the same. Hanging out simply means meandering through the universe in the company of friends. It takes place on park benches, in bleachers, or on a corner and involves no recognizable activity. Even physical movement can be at a minimum. You may pass a group of teenagers on a corner and return hours later only to find them in the same location, doing the same thing—apparently nothing!

This drives parents to distraction. They envision their child at sixty, still occupying the same corner with a group of graying cohorts who have accomplished nothing in their entire adult existence. Parents initiate dialogues in an attempt to understand the meaning of kicking back, but they usually generate more heat than light. A typical example follows:

The curious parent inquires, "Where are you going?"

Teenager grudgingly replies, "We're going out cruising."

"What does that mean?" demands the parent, who interprets this reply as evasion.

"It means just what I said!"

Desperate for clarity, the parent continues, "What are you going to do?"

"Just kick back."

Frustrated in their attempts to gain any meaningful information, parents often go on the offensive. "Doesn't anyone speak English anymore? Why do you kids waste your time just going down to the mall? Can't you think of anything better to do?" The explanation is usually, "It's fun, it's cool." The parent gives up the battle of words with a parting shot: "You'd better stay out of trouble!"

Sometimes teenagers give very vague answers about hanging out because they know their parents would disapprove of their actual plans, like driving to a mall in another part of town even though the parents have vetoed this idea on several other occasions.

The teenager's agenda for hanging out is to spend time with friends, talk, watch other teenagers, and just be together, separate from their families. It's not a meaningful activity in adult terms, but it is important to teens. Hanging out is a way that teenagers deal with stress. While they are with their friends, they can escape their worries about school and their futures, and the demands of their parents.

Hanging out allows teenagers to be children for a little longer. They can act silly, fantasize, and talk about life without adult judgment. Many serious, mature, successful adults look back with longing to the summer afternoons and evenings they spend lolling on the lawn with their friends.

The parent's reservations about hanging out include: Why are they wasting so much time? What are they up to? I don't feel in control when they are just out in the world being indolent. This leads some parents to worry and feel frustrated. However, parents who become good observers of their own behavior will see the value in the steps that follow.

FIRST STEP

You need to understand that every generation has its own form of hanging out. The malt shop, the corner drugstore, and the park were favorite sites in the past. Thinking about how you spent idle time with your friends when you were this age may help you sense the normality of this behavior.

SECOND STEP

Learn to become clearer about why you insist on asking, "Where are you going? What are you going to do?" I think these questions usually mean "What are you up to?" and "Stay out of trouble!" They are not the questions of a parent who is a good observer.

THIRD STEP

If you have a teenager who basically hangs out but doesn't get into trouble, say, "I want you to know that I really respect your judgment, even though you might just be going to the mall or driving around. I feel good about you because I can trust you. I know there must be times when you do things that I wouldn't like, but I don't think that happens very often and I still trust you."

By doing this you demonstrate a positive feeling about your teenager and even show acceptance of the fact that once in a while he or she might want to do small unacceptable things. This puts positive pressure on your teenager.

FOURTH STEP

You may have a teenager who isn't trustworthy and does whatever he or she wants even though you have objected to certain activities. In this case, you should say, "I wish I could trust you when you go out with your friends, but it's difficult because you don't always keep your promises. So now there will be a new rule.

"If I find out that you are doing things that you know I disapprove of, I will restrict the amount of time you can spend with your friends. I will increase the restriction by a day each time you don't follow the rules. I really hope that you don't make me do this."

Remember to increase the consequences consistently but in small increments. Let your teenager know that changing his or her behavior offers a chance to make things better. Increase the consequences to a week at a time if your teenager consistently disobeys or does something extremely inappropriate, such as driving to another town without asking or telling you.

4

ANTISOCIAL BEHAVIOR

"I'll never survive!"

Lying

Many parents believe that when their teenager lies it may be an indication of a character deficiency. They're also afraid that lying may have very serious consequences later in life if it is not dealt with vigorously. When parents discover that their teenager has been lying, they usually react like this: "Are you lying again? I can always tell when you're lying! You lie so much that I never know when to believe you anymore! There's nothing worse than a liar!"

Teenagers react in a number of ways. The bold ones look you straight in the eyes and say, "You lie, too! I hear you tell people on the phone that Dad's not home when he's standing right across the room! You used to tell Grandma we couldn't visit her because I had a cold just because you didn't like the things she let me do at her house."

The parent snaps back, "Don't get smart with me. Anyway, that's not the same. Those were white lies." The look on the teenager's face informs the parent that the kid isn't buying it!

A parent who is a good observer will respond like this: "You're right, I do lie sometimes. I should try not to be so negative when I talk to you about lying." In this way you take responsibility for your attitude but divert the discussion back to your concerns with your teenager.

Teenagers are old enough to know the implications of lying. They know that you see lying as wrong, and that they will get in trouble if they get caught. But most teenagers don't think that it is as serious a matter as you do, so they feel only mildly guilty about their lies. However, if they do something that is seriously wrong and they lie about it, they get very worried.

The main reason that teenagers lie is that it works. Lies frequently get them out of trouble or let them do what they want even if you disapprove. Lying during adolescence is very natural for some teenagers because of the need to have more and more control over their lives. Lies help them solve the conflict between their parents' rules and their need for autonomy. As they get older, they won't have to resort to lying because they will have more control.

The parents' agenda is to teach values and appropriate behavior, and lying doesn't qualify as a positive value to parents although teenagers see it differently. Parents see lying as a sign of a flawed character and are incensed that their kid would try to deceive them because it feels like a personal affront. How dare this kid try to outsmart me and think that it would work?

If you can remember that this is a developmental issue that will diminish and eventually disappear, it will help you to feel less anxiety. You will need to learn to react less negatively. When you react strongly to your teenager's lies, he will just learn to lie more effectively the next time so that you won't find out. I hope that I can give you some new ways to motivate your teenager to rely less on lying in dealing with you.

FIRST STEP

Think about how you approach your teenager concerning the issue of lying. Do you treat all lies the same, on principle? Do you assume that one lie leads to others, many others, and begin an inquisition? Don't treat lying like a major crime unless your teenager lies about something serious, like saying he or she is staying overnight with friends and then going someplace completely different.

The new approach is to help your teenager discover that rather than simply being angry, you are really concerned. By pointing out the implications of such behavior, you're trying to make clear that habitual lying can lead to a situation in which he or she would not be trusted.

SECOND STEP

If you are a parent who has overreacted to lying in the past, tell your teenager that you are going to try to handle his lying, like other issues, in a different way from now on. Even if you haven't overreacted, you should still say the following: "I was thinking how hard it is to tell the truth sometimes, even for adults. I realize that it's understandable to want to avoid dealing with some issues when you know you will get into trouble. Especially if I get upset. Even if I don't get upset, I know it's not always easy to tell the truth."

This lets your teenager know that you understand that the motives for lying are not always to deceive you but simply to avoid discomfort. This doesn't justify such actions but it shows that you understand that he isn't lying because he or she is a bad person.

THIRD STEP

Continue by telling your teenager, "I realize there are times when you lie to me and I don't find out, so you get away with something. Maybe that makes you feel like it's worth it to take the risk and lie. Lots of kids think that way. But I want you to know that I trust you, and I hope that you will use good judgment, even if you try to get around me once in awhile."

This kind of comment will surprise your teenager because it clearly shows that you are aware of his or her motives in justifying certain behavior.

FOURTH STEP

Tell your teenager, "I would really appreciate it if you would try not to lie to me, and I will try to be more understanding. I know there will be times when you will want to do something so bad that it will seem worthwhile to lie. But I hope you'll remember that you really have had the opportunity to do many things, and you will have more in the future, so I don't think that you should feel that you need to lie to me."

FIFTH STEP

In an effort to build a relationship of mutual trust, tell your teenager, "If you lie to me because you are in trouble or have done something

110

wrong, I really will try not to overreact when I find out. Even if you decide to tell me much later, I will respect you for making the effort to be honest, and I would prefer that to not telling me at all."

It may take some time for your teenager to trust you. The fear will be that in return for candor and honesty, you'll go crazy and ground him or her for years! Be patient. This approach really will help normal teenagers to be more truthful.

Frequent and Serious Lying

If you have a teenager who lies frequently and about more serious matters, you must take a different position.

FIRST STEP

Say to your teenager, "I really have tried to be understanding but I keep discovering that you lie to me about where you are going and other things. Trying to be understanding isn't working, so there will be new rules until you learn to be more truthful. I love you, but it worries me that you can lie so easily."

SECOND STEP

In a firm and supportive way tell your teenager, "I would rather not make tough rules to control your lying, but I am so concerned that I have no other choice. I really would like to know if you have any other way to solve this problem."

If he or she shows you a great deal of understanding and admits the severity of the problem, offer another chance prior to tough consequences. However, if you have been through this many times, proceed to the next step.

THIRD STEP

Explain to your teenager, "Every time I find out that you have lied to me, you will be grounded for one day and night on the weekend. That means no telephone calls and no visitors. If the family has plans to do something away from home, one of us will stay home with you while the others go out. If you continue to lie you will force me to double the grounding. That means you're going to miss a lot of fun if you don't learn to control your lying. For your own sake, I hope that you stop, and I really believe that you can."

Your strategy is to be firm, increase the consequences appropriately, but continue to show a great deal of understanding for the kid's feelings. Using this calm, firm approach, you give your teenager the message that it's his or her problem, not yours.

Stealing

Most teenagers rarely steal. Some will do a small amount of stealing, taking insignificant items from a store or taking things that they need or want from other people. This does not mean that they are preparing for a career as a thief, although many parents regard stealing as the first step on the road to the slammer!

Young children have a magical view of stealing, thinking that when they steal, no one sees them take anything. Older kids tend to feel that they just won't get caught. Teenagers, especially boys, like doing things such as stealing, because it's mildly dangerous. Successful stealing gives boys a feeling of power and importance, so they often brag to other boys about their heists. Girls usually just tell their closest friends.

Parents are extremely embarrassed by stealing because it goes against the norms of the community. Parents want to be seen to be teaching appropriate values and feel as if they are failing when they find out that their children are stealing. They can't believe that *their* child would dare to steal.

However, it's important for parents to understand that much of this behavior is another aspect of an adolescent developmental issue. Most teenagers experience the normal impulse to steal, to get something the easy way. Even teens who have all the things they need may steal because they want to know how it feels.

If parents have had good communication with their teenager, the chances are that he or she will be able to discuss the idea of stealing or admit to parents that something has been stolen. However, parents need to remember that some teenagers will go through their teens stealing occasionally, but never get caught. They usually stop around the age of seventeen or eighteen without any intervention from parents or law enforcement agencies.

Although it is true that much of teenage stealing is a developmental issue that will diminish in time, let's talk about how a parent should handle it.

FIRST STEP

If your teenager has never given you any reason to believe that she has stolen anything, take a few moments to have a discussion about the issue of stealing. In a calm setting, say to her, "I was thinking that one of the positive things about you is that you seem to have high standards of behavior. I have the feeling that you rarely if ever steal. In fact, I have no reason to think that you have stolen. I'm really just curious to know what you think about stealing, since I know that lots of kids do it from time to time.

"Even if you surprised me and said that you had stolen a few times, I'd still feel that basically you are a very honest person. I would still respect you and hope that you had learned from the experience." Most teenagers would be shocked if their parents were this understanding. This approach also reinforces your teenager's positive behavior.

SECOND STEP

If you have caught your teenager stealing a few times yet have little reason to believe that it happens on any regular basis, say the following in a calm voice: "I know [or suspect] that you have stolen from the store because I don't know of any other way that you could get those things. My main concern is not to make a huge issue of this, because I don't think that you do this very often. If I am right about the stealing, I really hope that you will stop doing it. If I am wrong and you haven't stolen anything, I apologize. It's just that this issue is very important to me because I believe that I must teach you to be a fair and honest person."

THIRD STEP

If you have caught your teenager stealing with some limited regularity and have strong suspicions or worries that this could be an ongoing problem, say the following: "I was thinking that I don't really know if you have stolen anything recently. I'm not accusing you, but I want you to know my feelings. I really love you, and I'm worried about this becoming a more serious problem.

"I'm afraid that you might think it's not a big deal to steal occasionally. But I do. It's easy to think that you'll never get caught. I think you're too good to do this again. I really want you to think about this because it's an extremely important issue to me."

FOURTH STEP

If you have a teenager who has been caught stealing on a regular basis, it is time to make your teenager understand that the behavior has to stop. Say to your teenager in a firm tone, "I really have tried to be understanding about this behavior, but if it happens again and I find out, you'll be grounded for a month. If you steal again after that, you will be grounded for two months."

Your teenager may say that this is not fair, that the punishment is too severe. Tell him or her, "I have told you before that it is extremely important to us that you learn the seriousness of stealing. You cannot minimize this behavior. I am being as fair as I can by telling you in advance what the consequence will be if you steal again. I need to convince you that it is very important to me that you stop stealing." You need to make it very clear to your teenager that stealing is more serious than other behaviors. Parents really make their point when they insist on a strong, unnegotiable consequence that is not a typical response.

Drugs and Alcohol

As teenagers gain more experience in the world, they learn that certain substances alter their physical and psychological experience of their surroundings. Drugs or alcohol can make them feel silly, mellow, brave, less inhibited, or more introspective. They may see drugs as a quick, reliable way to enhance their pleasure, feel more comfortable in social situations, or drown out all the negative feelings that frequently plague teenagers.

Another factor that makes substance abuse so compelling is peer pressure and the desire to be accepted. Teenagers want to be a part of their peer group. Being an outsider is a very difficult position for young people struggling to develop a positive self-image. Most teenagers are afraid that if they go to a party and don't take drugs, they will be rejected or seen as "uncool."

Despite the widespread efforts of such groups as the DARE (Drug

Abuse Resistance Education) project to change the perception of drugs as socially acceptable, the need or desire to experience drugs is still a strong aspect of adolescent development. It is not always easy to "Just say no."

The combination of drugs, alcohol, and teenagers scares parents to death! Even level-headed parents with good kids have fears and negative fantasies about their kids and substance abuse. Is he going to become crazy, weird, or an addict? Will she experiment with drugs and end up dead?

Parents who watch TV, read the newspaper, and listen to the news may be convinced that substance abuse has reached epidemic proportions. Still, although drug and alcohol abuse are major problems among the teenage population, in many cases parents' fears are much greater than reality warrants.

The reality is that more teenagers experiment with drugs or alcohol during their adolescence, but this is very different from being a regular drug user. There are some teens who never use any drugs, and others try drugs only once or twice. Some use a particular substance on a limited, regular basis all through adolescence and function relatively well. It is important to note that rarely do those teenagers develop serious drug problems, but that doesn't mean that parents should overlook this behavior or ignore the possibility of having a positive influence on the situation.

The agenda for the average teenager in experimenting with drugs and alcohol is to be a part of the peer group. They are also trying to emulate adult behavior and experience the physical sensation of being under the influence of some substance. Since many teenagers believe that they are invincible, they see little risk in this behavior. It is just another way to learn about the world on their own, despite strong parental disapproval.

It is understandable that parents become extremely worried about this issue because everything around them indicates that drug abuse could happen in their family. They become particularly alarmed when the teenager of friends is found to be on drugs. "He [she] seemed like such a good kid! How did it happen?" The parents' agenda concerning drugs is to make sure that their teenager doesn't do something that could totally ruin his or her life.

This leads many adults to resort to the FBI style of parenting. They institute routine checks of their teenager's room and car and observe his or her eyes and nose with great interest. Every sniff becomes an indication of drug use. Finally, if the investigative work uncovers enough circumstantial evidence, they may finally plan a drug bust in the kid's room, only to find him or her sleeping peacefully. All of this behavior is based on the parents' fear and inability to talk openly with the teenager about substance issues.

In this section, it is impossible to deal fully with the complicated problem of teenage substance abuse. If you have had good communication with your teenager up to this point, you may be able to bring up the topic of drugs from time to time. However, the subject may be difficult for any teenager to discuss with parents. I will try to advise you on ways to communicate with your teenager and influence his or her attitude toward substance abuse. I will also suggest rules to use if you discover that your teenager is using drugs or alcohol.

FIRST STEP

As a parent, what kind of behavior do you model concerning the use of pills (prescription or otherwise), alcohol, or drugs? Some parents see little similarity between their behavior and substance abuse, but there is a strong connection. Are you ready to accept the fact that your behavior and that of your friends plays a major role in influencing your teenager's attitude and behavior concerning substance abuse?

If your teenager sees you drinking regularly or using drugs at parties or family gatherings, it justifies his or her interest in experimenting with substances. It also renders your warnings about substance abuse hypocritical. Even if you are a mild but regular drinker, your teenager may feel entitled to challenge the consistency of what you do versus what you say.

SECOND STEP

If your teenager challenges your behavior, don't say "My drinking has nothing to do with this!" Avoid the impulse to say, "I don't drink or use drugs like you do!" These statements will destroy your credibility. You will also lose your ability to influence your teenager if you lecture about the evils of drugs in an emotional or irrational way.

When your teenager questions your behavior, I hope you will say, "You're right. I guess it's difficult for me to convince you to avoid drugs and alcohol if I drink." If you only drink socially on a limited basis, you can say, "I do like to drink occasionally at parties, so I can't criticize you for wanting to drink, too. But I hope you realize how serious taking drugs and drinking can be. I would give up drinking altogether if I thought I could convince you not to get involved with alcohol and drugs."

Some of you may be howling at this point, thinking that I am asking too much. Close the book! The guy's off the wall! Why should you give up your wine just because your kid's peer group wants to experiment with drugs? I would only suggest this if your teenager seems to have a serious substance abuse problem and your support and example could help the situation.

Parents who refuse to consider this type of action even if their teenager has a serious problem should take a hard look at their own patterns of behavior concerning substances. Their attitude may indicate that they have a problem with substances.

THIRD STEP

Take time to familiarize yourself with the symptoms of substance abuse. There are a number of changes in behavior that may indicate possible substance use. These include the need to sleep much of the time, grades going down over several semesters, and a general lethargy or hyperactivity. If a teenager who is usually talkative becomes withdrawn and is very reluctant to communicate, it can be an indication of drug abuse.

Remember that these are only *possible* indications of drug abuse, and this list of symptoms is certainly not complete. You seriously need to consider your responsibility to become better educated on the topic of substance abuse. Write to organizations such as the National Institute on Drug Abuse and ask for literature on the subject. I have suggested reading on this subject in the For Further Reading section at the end of this book.

FOURTH STEP

Don't wait for something to happen! Call your local community mental health center to find out when you can attend free discussions or lectures on the subject of drug abuse. Many hospitals offer this service.

After you know what is available, suggest to your teenager that you think it would be a good idea for both of you to be better informed about drugs. Say this in a positive way that tells your teenager that it's an important issue, and he or she is not being blamed for anything. Even if your teenager is in a school that has a program on drug awareness, a parent's interest is important because it creates the possibility for discussing drug abuse at home.

FIFTH STEP

Whether or not you have attended a meeting together, say to your teenager, "I know that most teenagers try drugs at some time. Even when I was a teenager, most kids tried drugs once or twice." If you have experimented with drugs, then you might say, "I tried drugs several times but I found that after awhile it really wasn't what I wanted to do. I realize that maybe you have, too. If I'm wrong, and you haven't tried drugs, that's great! The main thing I want to say is that I really believe that you have good judgment, and I hope you use it concerning drugs."

If your teenager says nothing, say, "I am only telling you this because I care about you and want to make sure you have thought about this issue." If your teenager has never tried drugs, he or she might say, "God, you don't trust me!" Just say you know that this is not an easy issue for either of you, but you have no reason not to trust him or her.

SIXTH STEP

If you find that your teenager doesn't have good judgment and has been using drugs or alcohol with some regularity, you need to say, "I have tried to help you understand my feelings about any use of substances. It seems to me that your situation is much more serious than just using drugs once in awhile or a few times."

If your teenager denies the seriousness of the situation or argues with you to minimize the problem, say, "No matter what you say, as a family we are going to get professional help. That's how much this concerns me. I can't let you continue doing something that may really hurt you because I care about you. There is not choice. We're going."

Continue to be understanding but extremely firm. Do not let your teenager minimize the danger of the situation. For very serious situations, refer to the Resources section at the end of this book.

SEVENTH STEP

The use of consequences will work if your teenager doesn't have a serious problem, but if there are patterns of drug use, consequences are not an appropriate remedy because they don't deal with the problem and may only send the behavior underground.

If you do use consequences, choose those that limit social contact with peers who are probably also using drugs. If you don't have this information, remember to use a consequence that is important to your teenager, such as no phone calls for a specific period of time, not going out on the weekend for a number of weeks, and so on.

If your teenager accepts limits, it means he or she is ready for boundaries. Although they may complain that they really want to get control of the situation themselves, many teenagers know you're right when you limit them concerning drugs. Even if they rarely admit it, they are relieved when you help them get control of themselves.

Smoking

Parents are understandably terrified about drugs and alcohol abuse, but smoking doesn't seem to create the same anxiety. Although smoking is a serious health issue, parents' concerns about teenage smoking tend to vary according to their own history with smoking.

Parents who smoke can't really convince their teenagers that smoking is dangerous any more than adults who drink are effective in discouraging teenagers from drinking. When kids are younger, they may listen to your advice regardless of your personal habits, but teenagers won't accept this inconsistency.

Teenagers' attitudes tend to be strongly polarized. They are either strongly opposed to smoking, or they smoke and deny the mass of evidence that says smoking is dangerous. It's not easy to impress teenagers with the reality of health risks that may not materialize for twenty years, because they generally believe that they're immortal or at least impervious to ailments and diseases, including cancer.

Teens who choose to smoke despite their parents' objections usually decide not to smoke around their parents, hiding the cigarettes and hoping that maybe their habit will never be discovered.

Although most parents would prefer that their teenagers not smoke, this issue doesn't usually become well focused. If your teenager insists on smoking and it bothers you, consider the following steps.

119

FIRST STEP

You need to be very clear about your own behavior and feelings on the subject of smoking. Do you worry about the long-term health risks for your child? Are you afraid he or she will fall asleep smoking and burn down the house? Do you just object because it seems unacceptable behavior? Your teenager doesn't need a lecture on the evils of smoking or occasional comments like, "Can't you break that ugly habit?" Most kids are aware of the health risks involved in smoking, and they may even see that it's an unattractive habit, but it feels sophisticated to smoke, which is much more important to teenagers than any other concerns.

SECOND STEP

Remember what was said about parental influence in other substance issues: The parents' behavior needs to be consistent with what they want from their teenagers. The same applies to the issue of smoking. You cannot demand behavior from your teenager that you refuse to model.

Sometimes education can be an effective way to influence your teenager's attitude toward smoking, especially if you suggest that you want to go together to a lecture on the effects of smoking. Tell her, "We'll just go once so that we can both be better informed. I know that you might think that this is unnecessary now, but I worry that you won't ever consider how important it is not to smoke."

If your teenager resists, say, "I would like to ask you again later on to go to a lecture with me. I hope you will consider how serious this issue is." If that doesn't work, drop it!

THIRD STEP

Although smoking is a serious health hazard, it's very difficult to stop or totally control this behavior because—unlike other drugs—the symptoms are easy to ignore and they don't create legal or psychiatric problems. Therefore drastic responses, such as enforcing serious consequences or staying upset for a long time, will not accomplish anything but give you a terrific headache. If you have tried modeling, education, and encouraging your teenager to quit smoking, you have to face the fact that your teenager will come to grips with this issue when he or she is ready.

Tell your teenager, "I realize that you're going to do what you want about smoking, and I can't really change that even if I think it's unhealthy. I guess you'll have to decide that for yourself when you are older. Maybe you think that I worry too much, and maybe you're right. It's just because you're so important to me."

FOURTH STEP

If you feel very strongly about the smoking issue, you can use consequences to try to discourage this behavior in your teenager, but accept the fact that the smoking will probably still go on behind your back. Nonetheless, you can have some control over the situation by designating areas and occasions where smoking is absolutely forbidden and setting consequences if you discover that your teenager is smoking.

In a firm but understanding tone of voice, say, "I object very strongly to smoking because it is a health hazard. You may not understand my insistence and you may feel mad at me, but I must insist that you absolutely do not smoke in the house or around the family. There are no exceptions to this.

"I don't want you to smoke at all, so if I find out that you have been smoking, there will be consequences. Your health concerns me so much that I am going to be very tough on this issue. If I discover that you have been smoking, I will not be responsive to any of your requests for assistance. That includes times when you need extra money or you want my help to do something special."

These are just examples of consequences, and by now you have probably figured out what works with your teenager.

Group Behavior of Teenagers

Many parents view the group behavior of teenagers as just a cut above that of wild animals! Making loud noises, running wild, chasing each other, and traveling in packs.

Teenagers cherish group behavior as one of the most enjoyable features of their adolescence, and despite what parents may have observed, it does have some beneficial aspects. During these years many teenagers establish friendships that will endure for a lifetime.

The negative but normal side of group behavior is that it stimulates the potential for testing authority, doing daring things, and bringing out the worst in each other. However, most of the time teenagers are just having fun and manage to limit their antics to those that just border on mild mayhem.

When teenagers go away in groups to such places as Palm Springs or Fort Lauderdale for spring vacation, the potential for negative behavior increases because they feel free of the shadow of adult authority.

In fact, most negative behavior takes place with friends or acquaintances and is usually limited to exhibitionism, being loud, or acting silly. This is because there are usually one or two kids in each group who act as the conscience for the whole group. And many groups of teens spend a lot of time together without any problems at all.

However, no matter how comfortable you are with your teenager's social group, most parents feel some concern about the potential for teenagers to get out of control when they are together. Here are some suggestions for dealing with your concerns about group behavior and building communication with your teen.

FIRST STEP

Try to assess the quality of your teenager's friends. What are they like? If you don't know, you must become more observant. Are they impulsive? Do they use poor judgment? Are they irresponsible? Does your teen share these characteristics to a disturbing degree? If you answered yes to these questions, there is potential for some problems with group behavior.

SECOND STEP

This is a good topic for an open discussion about your teen's view of his or her friends and their behavior when they are together. You need to do this without lecturing or having a long-drawn-out conversation. Start the conversation by saying, "I was wondering what it's like when you go out with your friends in a group." Your teenager may think, "What is she getting at? She's being too nice about this. I think I'm going to get trapped!"

Say, "I'm really just interested. I'm not trying to find out if your friends are doing anything wrong." You must say this very positively; your objective is to build communication, not nail the kid. "Is it difficult to keep Jim in control? He gets pretty wild here at the house. Some kids come close to getting in trouble. Does that ever happen to your group?" A note of caution: Your attitude must be casual and interested, not probing. If you hear something even mildly upsetting, say, "I'm glad you were able to tell me. So you think you could have gotten into trouble?"

At this point your teenager may not say anything, may disagree, or may continue the conversation in the way that you hope. Much of this depends on your attitude and tone. No matter what the response, say, "I really hope you are the one in the group who uses good judgment, because sometimes I worry about what you and your friends might do when you are together." With many normal teens, these dialogues help them to see that you are understanding and accepting, and this encourages them to think about their behavior. Always remember to give praise for being open with you.

THIRD STEP

If your teenager and a group of friends have been involved in trouble a number of times, follow this approach. Say, "I've made a new rule. Before you go out again with your friends, I want to meet with all of them at our house to discuss what I expect of everyone, not just you. Otherwise, you can't go out with the group."

Your teenager might say, "Are you joking? I can't believe you'd do that to me." You may want to blurt out, "Don't get smart with me. I'm your parent!" but instead try saying, "I understand that it would be a little embarrassing. So what can we come up with as an alternative?" Here you are negotiating with him to find a solution that is mutually agreeable.

Your teenager may offer, "I promise not to get into any trouble, and I will talk to my friends." Your reply should be to accept the solution with a qualification: "We'll try that but if there's one more incident, you'll have to do it my way. I hope your method works."

FOURTH STEP

If another incident occurs, use this approach. Remember, don't say, "You promised me! I can never believe anything you say!" Instead, firmly tell him, "You will have to tell your friends that you can't go out with them for the next two weeks. And I will have to meet with all of them at the house before you can go out with them again."

Don't lecture or discuss this issue at this point. Tell him, "It's your responsibility to talk with your friends and arrange a time when they can come over. I realize that's not easy, but it's my rule."

FIFTH STEP

When the group has gathered, tell them, "I don't know how much your parents know, but I am meeting with you because you have been getting into trouble recently. I like you as a group and I know that Jim really likes to be with you, but if you can't stay out of trouble, you will be seeing less and less of him. So you guys can't go out next weekend.

"I don't know if your parents are aware of what has been going on, and for now I don't care. This is between us. But if there is another incident, I am going to talk to all of your parents." If it is a serious problem, you should not wait to take action. "I really hope you don't force me to do this. I would prefer that you take care of this by yourself. That's all. No long lecture. You can go now."

If your teenager goes out with people who are not close friends and you can't get them together, adapt these ideas for him or her alone. This approach lets all of them know that you are fair, reasonable, and understanding but firm.

Negative Peer Pressure

When kids become teenagers, the physical and emotional power that parents have over them diminishes considerably. Many parents are disturbed by this feeling of loss of control and fear the influence that seems to have replaced them—peer pressure. In most cases, peer influence is not fraught with disaster but involves such stunts as sneaking into a theater without paying or buying beer illegally.

But adults often imagine far more serious events and feel scared. Parents tend to handle this issue as follows: "You're so easily influenced by Cindy. You'd do anything that she tells you to do. Why do you listen to her? When you're with those kids you act like you don't have a mind of your own! Why don't you find some friends that are as good as you?"

Any normal teenager will respond in self-defense. "I'm not doing anything because Cindy tells me to. You just don't understand." She will probably also think, "She has her nerve. Some of her friends are a lot worse than mine!"

Peer pressure is something all teenagers face, but for most of them there are no serious negative effects. But all parents worry about the influence of the wrong kind of kid or group. At some time it may seem that their teenager has chosen or been pressured into taking the wrong path, cutting classes to go to the beach, or crashing a party without being invited. They wonder if the kid can stand up to her friends without feeling rejected. Does he or she share your values or is the opinion of the group more important?

While the issue of peer pressure may make you very anxious, remember that by showing your negative feelings about your teenager's friends you are giving out the message that you think he or she can be easily influenced and can't make proper decisions alone. This will simply make the kid feel more protective about his or her choice of friends and the things they want to do.

To help you realize how your criticism affects your teenager, imagine how you would feel if your spouse or relative said, "You never listen to a thing I suggest, but you'll take advice from everyone else. What's the matter with you?"

There are many occasions when teenagers must handle peer pressure, many of which you will never know about. How can you have a positive influence against the negative pressure of friends, acquaintances, and role models?

Think about your teenager's behavior with friends. You may be fortunate enough to have a teenager who is independent and resourceful and has shown very little indication of being troubled by peer pressure. If so, you can have an open dialogue about this issue. If you feel that your teenager is easily influenced in a negative way by peers, you will need a different approach.

FIRST STEP

If your teenager appears to be rather independent, you might say, "I've noticed that you don't seem to be easily influenced by your friends when they are doing something that you don't want to do. Am I right? I want you to know that being able to make up your mind is a great trait that's going to help you all through your life; no one will be able to influence you to do things that aren't in your best interest." In this way you reinforce your teenager's positive traits and have an opportunity to restate your values.

SECOND STEP

If you have been very critical of the influence that your teenager's friends seem to have, say, "I don't think I've been very clear with you when we have talked about how your friends influence your attitudes and behavior. It might have sounded critical, but really I think I just worry that you might not be able to stand up to your friends if they try to convince you to do something that's not right. I need to learn to ask you if you feel you are easily influenced rather than telling you that you are.

"I will try to respect your view on this issue. I wonder how hard it is to resist the other kids when they want to do something that is wrong." By asking the question in this way, you allow your teenager to talk with you about this on equal terms instead of saying that he or she doesn't know what he's doing.

THIRD STEP

You may have observed that your teenager has been negatively influenced by friends, or you may have been told by someone you trust that your teenager was seen participating in socially unacceptable behavior. He may have been asked to leave a football game because of rowdy behavior, or she and her friends may have been teasing or tormenting other kids in a very cruel way.

Tell your teenager, "Mrs. Harvey saw you and your friends teasing that new kid in the neighborhood." Don't follow up by raising your voice, shaking your head, and inquiring in disbelief, "How could you do that? How could you be so mean and unfeeling? That's not the way I raised you!"

Instead say, "It really makes me feel sad that you and your friends, but particularly you, treat another kid that way. I really think of you as a nice kid and I don't believe that you're like that. I'm really disappointed that you could be influenced to be so mean to someone. It makes me think that you haven't really learned how important it is to be kind to other people. I know that you're a better kid than that, and I hope you'll promise not to do that again. It's important to me and your dad that you know how to treat other people."

If you have a teenager who is basically good and treats people well, this approach doesn't judge but appeals to the best part of your child from the best part of you.

FOURTH STEP

If you have a teenager who has a pattern of being negatively influenced by peers, you need to say, "I don't want to do this but I will because I think the situation is serious enough to warrant it. If you can't behave better when you are with your friends, they will all have to come over and talk to me. I'll tell them in front of you that if you don't improve your behavior, you won't be allowed to spend time together."

Tell your teenager that if the others refuse to do this, he or she simply won't be able to spend any more time with them. Also, if the behavior persists, you will ask the parents to get together and discuss the situation. Sometimes mild social embarrassment is very effective in changing teenagers' behavior without being demeaning.

Behavior at School

Teenagers are sentenced to twelve years of hard labor in school, years that they feel would be better spent lolling at the beach, going to parties, or listening to music. Thus, since school is frequently not on their preferred list, problems may develop that require parental intervention.

It can be a strange and uncomfortable experience for most parents to go to their teenager's school. These visits stir memories of their own high school career, along with the anxiety of meeting with teachers and hearing the bad news—since it's usually bad news that brings parents to school. Their teenager may have been caught cutting class, leaving campus, or being disrespectful or disruptive in class. The parents' reaction is often panic, anger, and then embarrassment.

Parents and teenagers frequently have this kind of discussion when there is trouble at school: "You better get your act together! At the rate you're going, you'll still be in high school at twenty-five. I'm not sending you to school for a vacation or a degree in delinquency."

When a teenager gets in trouble at school for such things as cheating on a test, talking back to the teacher, being tardy, or leaving school unexcused, the agenda is to keep the news from parents for as long as possible. I'll get killed if they find out, so I'll just forge their signatures. If I lie they'll be mad; if I don't they'll be furious. Maybe

I'll go live on another planet, or I could just hide under the covers. The objective is to avoid the problem at all costs.

The parents' agenda is to see that their teenager gets a good education and doesn't shame them, so when the school calls, they panic, then get mad, and finally deal with the problem. Most of the time the problem isn't nearly as bad as they first feared. But teenagers need to learn that inappropriate behavior at school has to stop. Here are some steps to help you solve the problem.

FIRST STEP

Make an effort to keep in regular contact with your teenager's teachers, before problems develop. A call or note once a month can be an excellent preventive measure. If you are positive and sincerely interested, teachers will usually be very responsive to your inquiries. Tell the teachers that you are concerned about your child's progress and would be grateful to know if any help is needed or if any difficulties are showing up.

SECOND STEP

Be aware of how you approach a teenager who is in trouble. If you really want to solve school problems, try to communicate in this way. Say, "I will try very hard not to be mad at you. But I really want to find out how you can solve this problem and see that it doesn't happen again. If you can tell me why you have been having trouble in school, I will be glad to listen. If you can think of a way to solve this problem, I am willing to consider your ideas and try them."

THIRD STEP

If your teenager has had only minor problems in school, you should talk to the teacher and tell your teenager that you are going to have regular contact with his or her teachers for the next three months. Arrange to meet or talk to the teachers about twice a month. Tell your teenager, "I am doing this because I am concerned about you. Once I see that you are doing better, I will stop checking on you."

FOURTH STEP

If your teenager has had regular problems in school, again talk to the teachers, and agree on a system for checking on your teenager's behavior. Have your teenager get the signature of each teacher at the end of the week, indicating if there has been any problem during the week. Continue this for one semester. This shows that you intend to have control over the situation, even if you aren't at school.

FIFTH STEP

Tell your teenager that if he or she doesn't solve the problems at school and stay out of trouble, there will be a consequence that will increase each time that there is any trouble. For example, since school behavior is very important, the consequence should be something that is very important to your teenager. You might want to double the consequence each time there is a recurrence of the problem until your teenager realizes that you are very concerned about school performance. For example, "Every week you get into trouble at school, you will be grounded for one weekend. If it occurs again you will be grounded for two weekends, and the next time it will be three." In this way your teenager learns that this is extremely serious to you.

SIXTH STEP

If your teenager continues to have behavior problems at school even after you have tried this method, you should consider seeing a counselor. This will again reinforce that this behavior must stop.

5

ATTITUDES AND FEELINGS

"Why do you make me feel so crazy?"

Arguing

One of the most common complaints that I hear from parents centers on the frustration they experience in dealing with their teenagers who insist on arguing relentlessly about everything. This form of verbal combat increases as kids get older because they have greater verbal skills and are more experienced in dealing with you. There are also many more things that they are willing to argue about.

Many teenagers develop formidable verbal skills that help them in school and will be very useful later in their careers, but they can make their parents' lives miserable. In other words, the kid has a big mouth and always has an answer. With one who started arguing early, the skill is sharply honed by puberty. Now the kid is an expert on everything!

Many parents find themselves arguing endlessly with their teenager over even minor points, and finally out of exasperation they scream, "Don't argue with me! I'm the parent!" The teenager says to himself, I'm arguing? What do you think you're doing? You're supposed to be the mature one. Teenagers who are observant like to say, "What about the way you and Dad argue? I didn't know there was any other way of communicating!"

130

The point that I am trying to make is that parents have to become better observers of their own behavior and develop better self-control about arguing. It may help you to keep in mind that your teenager is not trying to ruin your life. When your teenager argues, it means, "I want my way, but I'm too mature to throw a physical tantrum, so I will state my case with a verbal tantrum. If I don't get my way, you're going to hear about it and hear about it and hear about it."

Parents argue with their teenagers for a number of reasons, but primarily to communicate their values. They also argue to make them understand their rules, expectations, and worries about their welfare. These are all very positive motivations. Unfortunately, when they are expressed during an argument, they often just lead to more disagreements and misunderstandings.

Some teenagers present valid observations and fair arguments, so they feel that their parents should treat them with more respect since they know what they are talking about. Unfortunately, some parents seem to have an unwritten rule—never admit the teenager has a valid point. This only increases the arguing because the teenager doesn't feel understood. For example, a teenager may say, "I think I'm old enough to decide which college I want to attend." Their parents may say in a questioning tone, "How thoroughly have you checked into any of the colleges? Don't just go there because all of your friends are going." The teenager immediately feels that his or her judgment has been invalidated.

Before we attempt to solve the problem of the endless argument, let's look at a typical argument between parents and their teenagers:

> "What do you mean, I can't go to Erick's party? Everyone's going! You let my brother go to parties all the time when he was a sophomore!"
> "That's not true and I already told you that you can't go. I don't want to discuss it."
> "You never let me do anything, and you always say I'm wrong. You're not fair!"
> "I'm not saying you're wrong, but you can't go. I let you do lots of things but it's never enough. You always want more."
> "I still don't see why I can't go."
> "If you don't shut up, I'm going to blow my top! I don't want to hear another word! Is that clear?"
> "But . . ."

131

If this dialogue seems painfully familiar to you and you're sick of arguing, giving in, or winning but feeling upset, consider the steps that follow to handle arguments in a different way.

FIRST STEP

You may be thinking, What am I supposed to do? Just listen and take that barrage lying down? To change your pattern of arguing, you need to first look at how often you argue with your teenager. If you regularly engage in arguments, you are probably a major part of the problem. You may think that you're just trying to make your point but your efforts just fuel the argument.

Ask yourself why you continue to argue with your teenager. Part of the answer is that you feel that you should be listened to because you're the parent. You probably also argue out of frustration and because you have failed to notice that it doesn't work!

SECOND STEP

If you have experienced a great deal of frustration in arguing with your teenager, you need to observe yourself carefully. Do you really take the time to listen to what your teenager says, or do you just react at the first sign of resistance or difficulty?

Say to your teen in a calm moment, "I really would like to see if we can stop arguing so much. I'll try to listen to your ideas, and I hope that you will try not to argue so much. Let's talk about how we are doing in a couple of weeks."

If this problem isn't chronic, just having this talk can be helpful because it creates a positive way of focusing on the problem.

THIRD STEP

If you have a teenager who doesn't respond to your overtures or just becomes more insistent about arguing a point, consider trying this: In any discussion, make your point *no more than twice*. After that, if your teenager continues to argue, say, "It doesn't sound like anything I can say will help us understand each other. So I am not discussing this anymore." (And really stop!)

Unless your teenager says something that makes you rethink your position, firmly and empathetically say, "It sounds like you'll only feel better if I agree with you, but sometimes I just don't."

FOURTH STEP

If you have a teenager who just doesn't stop arguing with you even when you are clear and understanding, this is the next step. Make your point and walk away, even if your teenager keeps arguing. Many times this stops the behavior because it's no fun to argue by yourself! If you just refuse to respond, your teenager will eventually stop. Some parents are saying, "This guy doesn't know my kid. It will never work." With hardened cases, that's probably true, so here's the next step.

FIFTH STEP

Say to your teenager, "I have really been trying not to argue with you, but it seems like you just can't stop, so this is my rule. I'll warn you to stop arguing once. If you don't, I'll tell you to stop once. If you refuse to stop, there will be a consequence. It will increase each time you argue until you learn to stop. Unless you get control of yourself, you're going to lose a lot of free time. I hope you will consider that." Remember that consequences are most effective when they are meaningful to the teenager.

SIXTH STEP

You can help the situation improve by noticing any positive change in the situation. Try to recognize and reinforce any effort your teenager makes to control the arguing. You can say, "I noticed that you're trying to stop arguing, and I really appreciate it. I realize it's not easy, so I want to thank you." Your teenager may think you're delirious when you do this, but don't let this distract you from continuing with the new approach.

Also, validate any good point that your teenager makes by saying, "Even though you have to do what I tell you, you have made some valid points, such as the fact that I don't always listen to you and that I'm not always fair. I'm going to think about those issues and we'll talk more later." This makes clear that even though the arguing has to stop, you are really listening to and willing to consider the kid's point of view.

Moodiness

Once upon a time you had a happy, friendly kid in your house. He or she had an outgoing personality and seemed genuinely to like you. You could count on the kid to be cheerful and enthusiastic about family activities, and seemingly with life in general.

Then one day around the age of thirteen, a personality transplant seemed to have taken place. That sunny disposition was replaced by a sullen creature who seemed to be perpetually in the depths of winter—glum, gloomy and dismal. Teenage moodiness has struck!

The symptoms of moodiness include rarely smiling, acting annoyed when parents attempt to communicate, expressions of boredom, and a staunch refusal to show joy, no matter what! Responses are made in a scarcely audible voice or snarled at full volume. Then, without warning, your adorable girl or boy reappears, probably because someone smiled at her or him in school. But don't start celebrating because the moodiness may return as quickly as Superman can change clothes in a telephone booth.

Parents may wonder if the kid is manic-depressive. Guess again. This is just part of the normal teenage struggle to understand life. Your teenager is probably as puzzled by these moods as you are. No matter how annoying and unnecessary this moodiness seems, it is truly a developmental phase that will pass, and that friendly kid who likes you will reappear.

Parents must be careful not to overreact to this normal moodiness. Out of frustration they will sometimes say, "What's wrong?"

"Nothing!"

"You've been in a bad mood for two weeks and it's time for you to snap out of it!"

Your teenager feels criticized and reacts defensively, "I'm not moody! Leave me alone! You never understand me."

Parents with normal feelings are stung by the little ingrate and say, "If you think I'd ever do anything for you with an attitude like that, you'd better think again." When parents are not good observers, they simply aggravate the situation and the moodiness continues.

Teenagers, on the other hand, don't understand all the confusing feelings they're having because they aren't old enough or experienced enough to analyze what's bothering them. Teenagers often feel upset or worried about boy- or girlfriend problems, school, peer pressure, parental expectations, or the future. Teenagers can also feel intense pain or pleasure about romantic fantasies, and this contributes to major mood swings.

These are complicated feelings that create many, many moods. Your kid isn't weird, just frequently bewildered by a flood of new emotions and concerns and probably wondering why no one ever said that growing up would be so difficult and confusing. If he or she had the insight, you would hear, "Mom and Dad, please try to understand that I'm not really a snotty kid. I'm just mixed up, and I need to sulk until I get older and learn to handle these feelings."

The parents' agenda is usually to encourage, cajole, or threaten the teenager out of this moodiness because they feel that the behavior is inappropriate and annoying. The moodiness makes some parents uncomfortable and worried, so they become overly concerned and think that their teenager is suffering from depression.

Parents need to develop a great deal of empathy for this struggle and not take it personally when a teenager is moody. Remember that this emotional turmoil is an essential part of growing up.

At this point I must caution you that there is a difference between teenagers who are periodically moody and those who are rarely happy. If your teenager is continually moody, it certainly can be a signal that professional help is needed. But most parents are dealing with normal moodiness and just want to be helpful, so here are some suggestions for getting you through this period.

FIRST STEP

You need to work on accepting the fact that the most likely explanation for your teenager's moodiness is that it's part of an attempt to deal with certain feelings without knowing how. Observe your own response. Stop reacting personally to your teenager's moodiness and try to remember it usually has nothing to do with you.

SECOND STEP

Tell your teenager, "I've been thinking how I feel when you're in a bad mood or seem to be depressed, and I realize that I need to be more understanding when you are not feeling happy. I get into bad moods, too and I know it's not fun. I'll try not to accuse you of being moody anymore, because I think that just annoys you." This really begins to help the teenager to feel understood instead of criticized and judged.

135

THIRD STEP

If you have never been negative or critical of your teenager, skip the second step and start by saying, "I really wish I could help you when you don't seem very happy. I can see that it's hard for you to talk right now, but I hope that sometimes you'll talk to me when you're un-happy, because it might help and I really love you very much."

If this produces a positive response and you see indications that the talking helped, say, "It really feels good to finally be able to help a little with the things that are upsetting you. I hope you won't mind if I approach you when you are upset and we can do this again."

FOURTH STEP

If you have an unresponsive teenager who says nothing or acts nega-tively toward you, say, "It makes me sad that I can't help you when you seem upset. I hope sometime you will be able to come to me when you feel unhappy. I really think it's difficult to handle feelings alone all the time. If you have to do it that way, I'll understand, but I hope you'll find out how much talking can help when you're feeling bad."

FIFTH STEP

You would only use a consequence over this issue if your teenager's attitude was extremely negative toward you. In most cases, again, this is not intentional but just more evidence of the struggle with feelings. The parent's job in this area is to show a great deal of understanding. I hope the examples in this section demonstrate how caring you can be to your teenager concerning the complicated moods that he or she is experiencing.

Attitude Toward Parents: Tone of Voice, Dirty Looks, Criticism, and Sarcasm

When children are young, they make faces, talk sarcastically, or say silly things to let adults know that they are upset with them or the events in their lives. When they become teenagers, they display their displeasure through a nasty tone of voice, dirty looks, and sarcastic comments. These performances become so refined that you would swear that they had taken a seminar in Outstaring Parents or Master-ing Sarcasm.

Parents usually interpret this behavior as disrespect and handle it in a variety of ways. Some ignore it most of the time unless they are having a bad day or a particularly well-aimed remark hits home. Then they explode with remarks such as, "You'd better change your tone when you talk to me. You're not too old to be slapped," and with that the behavior usually subsides for a time.

Other parents, who tend to be more philosophical and tolerant, just accept that it is part of teenage behavior and look forward to the day when it will end or the kid will go away to college, whichever comes first.

In some families, this style of interacting is normal for all members, not just the teenagers. Parents model criticism, sarcasm, or glaring as a means of communicating, and the kids just follow suit. In these situations the behavior doesn't usually disappear as the teenager matures but becomes a part of his or her adult behavior.

A continuing theme in this book has been the need for teenagers to establish their identities separate from their parents. One way they do this is by expressing developing ideas and values that may not be shared by their parents. They usually inform their parents of the difference between their values by displaying annoyance with the parent's attitudes. All those remarks that make you feel like a dinosaur are actually intended to define the separation between you and them. But since the process of separation is largely unconscious, teenagers are rarely aware that their tone of voice and remarks have become offensive.

Sarcasm, dirty looks, and critical remarks are also ways that teenagers can safely express aggression and anger. For example, if a teenager is unhappy with something that his parents have said or done, a snotty look is a way of getting back at them without getting in a lot of trouble.

Teenagers also use these same tactics with their peers. They express their competitive feelings through constant taunting, teasing, and cutting remarks, sometimes to the applause of onlooking friends. Some of this behavior is transferred to their interactions with adults, who tend to be offended rather than amused.

If this behavior springs from complicated family problems or the teenager feels very troubled, the following approach might control but not resolve the behavior. With most teenagers the steps that I suggest will help a great deal.

FIRST STEP

Notice if you have been ignoring this behavior too much, allowing it to become excessive, or if you have been overreacting when it should just be ignored. Both of these reactions only aggravate the situation by giving your teenager power over you. This has to change!

SECOND STEP

Start by saying in a calm moment, "I wonder if you have noticed that you tend to look at me and talk in a very irritated way. I'm not bringing this up to criticize you, but I would like to give you one example in case you don't know what I'm talking about. I know that sometimes I react badly to you and we both get upset, so I would like us to work on this."

THIRD STEP

Tell your teenager, "I should have found a better way in the past to let you know that you really need to be aware of the way you talk to me. From now on when you give me a dirty look or use a negative tone of voice, I'm going to remind you. But I'll try to do it in a positive way."

The next time your teenager gives you a dirty look, say, "This is one of those times when you look and sound annoyed. Could you try to talk to me differently? I'd really appreciate it." Some of you may be howling in disbelief. "My kid is acting like a snot, and he wants me to say that?" Yes, because it's the only way that you'll find out if your teenager is willing to change his attitude.

If your teenager responds, don't forget to say how much this helps the situation, and that you appreciate the effort.

FOURTH STEP

If you have a teenager who doesn't respond positively and persists in a negative pattern, say, "I have tried to tell you in a nice way that you have to work on changing your expression and tone of voice. If you don't try harder, I plan to ignore anything you say and anything you are asking for when you use that tone. If you want to be heard, you'll have to pay attention to how you sound." These steps usually curb occasional outbursts. If this fails to improve the situation, move to the next step.

FIFTH STEP

Move to this plan of action only if there is persistent negative behavior. If there has been no positive change, say, "Your attitude is still troubling me and it has to change. I don't want to feel angry at you over this any more than you do. So I want you to think about a way that you can control this behavior. If you don't, there will have to be a consequence. I would prefer not to do that, but I will if you can't get control of yourself."

Remember to use systematic consequences that are meaningful to your teenager and increase in severity if the behavior persists.

Those Embarrassing Parents

Because parents frequently see their children as extensions of themselves, their behavior, particularly in public, is closely monitored. Parents want their children to reflect positively on them—a small reward for all their efforts. So you often hear parents trying to correct anything that will embarrass them. "Don't act that way. You're embarrassing me!" "Why are you wearing that terrible outfit? It doesn't match." "Don't laugh so loud."

Well, usually around thirteen or fourteen, teenagers become extremely self-conscious about their images and see their parents as an extension of that image. So the tables are suddenly turned. The concerned parent suddenly becomes the object of concern as the teenager tries to refine the parent into a more acceptable public person. This process usually includes comments on clothing, behavior, and any other eccentricity that the teenager finds embarrassing. "You look funny in that outfit, Mom." "Don't hug me in front of my friends. It's so embarrassing. I'm not a little kid." "Mom, don't say hi to Mrs. Schwartz. She'll know that I like her son."

The parent usually responds with, "Don't be ridiculous. How would she know that? And stop telling me what I should wear. I've been dressing myself for forty years without your help." This protest makes no difference to the teenager who is probably thinking of other comments such as, "Do you have to laugh so loud? You're acting like a teenager. And could you wait in the car when you come to pick us up?"

The teenager's agenda is to be accepted and always look appropriate, and never seem foolish or be associated with anything that doesn't fit their values. Parents can unintentionally become a great source of embarrassment and discomfort for teenagers, who deal with their embarrassment by rejecting their parents' style, attitude, or values. This is another way that they become separate and establish their individual identities.

Teenagers begin to observe and evaluate the way their parents handle themselves in comparison to other adults. For example, they may notice that the parents of a friend are more athletic, keep in better shape, and act younger. Your teenager may come home one day and say, "God, Anthony's parents are really cool. They go jogging twice a week and play tennis. Why don't you take better care of yourself?" You may try to ignore such remarks, but you're thinking that if you have to hear one more report about Anthony's healthy parents, you'll need a week in bed.

On the other hand, you may feel hurt and criticized by this kind of remark, but usually your teenager does not intend to be mean. Comparisons and evaluations of parents help teenagers to understand who their parents are and also to clarify their own likes and dislikes. However, some teenagers criticize their parents because they have been allowed to do this from an early age. These teens need consequences to change their behavior.

As your teenager grows up, their need to criticize becomes less important as they become more comfortable with themselves and begin to understand who their parents really are. If parents react negatively to this behavior, it may last considerably longer. Understanding the meaning of comparisons and criticism may keep you from taking their remarks too personally. Although your feelings may be hurt occasionally, try to remember that this is one of the basic ways that teenagers develop their own identities.

FIRST STEP

Remember that your teenager is easily embarrassed. Think about whether your teenager acts like this once in awhile or has fallen into the habit of criticizing you. If it happens only occasionally, say nothing and it will pass. If it happens often, you should start with the following approach:

SECOND STEP

Say, "I don't think you realize that some of the things you say to me sound very critical. For example, you say, "God, Mom, that outfit is too young for you! You look silly."

If your teenager says, "So what? You talk like that to me!" or just looks annoyed, you should say, "I know you don't like to hear these things, but the next time it happens I'll point it out to you. I really need you to try to stop talking to me in such an annoyed and bossy way."

THIRD STEP

Say to your teenager, "I realize that some of the things I do may annoy or embarrass you. I will try to be sensitive to your feelings, but you need to try to be more understanding about the things that you find annoying about me.

"If you can learn to point out the things that embarrass you in a nice way, I will consider your comments. I'll try to be more aware of your feelings, particularly if your concern involves your friends, because I know that you are easily embarrassed when they are around. But I won't always agree with your remarks and in those cases, I'll tell you as nicely as possible."

FOURTH STEP

If you have a teenager who continues to be critical and show disapproval of you, you should say in a strong tone, "I have tried to tell you nicely that I want you to stop making critical comments. From now on if you don't try harder, I will have to tell you in a way that you won't like! I hope you don't let it get to that point." Let your teenager know that you are appropriately annoyed.

If this doesn't work, move to a consequence such as, "The next time you talk to me like that, you will lose time with your girlfriend." Remember to use any consequence that is meaningful to your teenager, and increase the consequences until the negative behavior decreases.

Fears and Worries

Teenagers today face many new fears and difficulties in addition to the typical worries we all experienced as we were growing up. In addition to the usual concerns about succeeding in school, making friends, family problems, and planning for the future, teenagers are acutely aware of AIDS and other sexually related diseases. They have an increased concern about violent crime, personal injuries, and the threat of nuclear war. This is a heavy burden for anyone to carry.

Teenagers are bombarded with information about these issues through television, radio, and the print media. Sometimes they cope with this negative avalanche by denying that the problems exist. They may also cope by believing that they are immune to these dangers. Their grandiose feeling of power lets them believe that nothing can touch them so they'll live forever.

Although parents may be annoyed or amused by the unreality of these feelings, wanting to deny worries and fears is not just a teenage impulse. If you stop to think about it, adults often react in the same way, denying feelings and situations that are simply too overwhelming to face. Adults routinely deny that they have serious drinking problems, marital difficulties, or unmanageable situations with in-laws or children.

Some teenagers are so convincing in their denial that their parents believe that nothing bothers them. This apparently carefree attitude causes anxiety for parents who feel that kids should have some awareness and concern about the difficult aspects of growing up. Thus they lecture their teenagers on the dangers of the world: drugs, swindlers, violence, and unemployment. This lecture usually falls on deaf ears as the teenager impatiently wonders how many times he has to hear this "scary story about the world out there." The parent is trying to find out if the teenager worries enough to use good judgment, but unfortunately this only strengthens the denial.

Despite the unworried image that your teenager may be displaying, it is important to remember that all teenagers have many feelings that are unexpressed. It's not possible or realistic to assume that any parent can deal with all of these problems. But they can give their teenagers the message that they are aware of the issues and care about their feelings.

Maturity will take care of some of these issues, but an understanding parent sets a tone for the teenager's life. One of the most reassuring feelings a teenager can have is the certainty that his or her parents will be there to talk whenever needed. Parents can teach their teenagers that they may not always be able to solve everything in life, but they can feel understood.

FIRST STEP

Think about the fact that adults often find it difficult to talk about their fears and worries. How many times has an obviously upset friend told you that nothing was wrong? If you remember that adults have trouble with this, it will help you understand that your teenager will find it even more difficult unless your family has learned to talk about feelings and fears with each other.

SECOND STEP

In a quiet moment, there are things you can say to help your teenager deal with these fears and feel understood. Say, "I was thinking about how hard it was when I was your age to deal with worries about my future and being afraid of things that were going on in the world. I wonder if you feel any of these things?"

If your teenager responds positively, then you can start occasional dialogues that will help to relieve normal anxieties. Parents need to learn that just feeling understood is sometimes more important than having solutions to problems.

THIRD STEP

If your teenager looks puzzled or doesn't seem to respond, you can say, "Well, I'm just concerned, and I want you to know that even if you don't want to talk, I'm always interested." Try hard not to react to the lack of response.

FOURTH STEP

Periodically, it is helpful to come back to your teenager and say, "I just want to check in with you, in case you've been thinking about anything that worries or scares you." Just your continuing interest is meaningful to your teenager during this difficult time. Even if he or she thinks that you are weird for talking about these things, your concern will still be appreciated.

Unhappiness

Unhappiness is a normal human emotion that all of us experience throughout our lives, but as a rule it lasts for relatively short periods of time and then we regain our emotional balance. Young children can be very unhappy one moment and, the next thing you know, they're back to their usual cheerful selves. Adults tend to hide their unhappiness because they have to function in a personal and social world where such feelings generally are not expressed.

Teenagers are not yet subject to the social restrictions of adults. They brood when they are unhappy, presenting a very somber face to the world and rarely smiling despite your best efforts to cajole them into a better mood. They actually enjoy being alone and listening to sad music that only increases their misery. Indulging in feelings of unhappiness and playing "poor me" are part of the process of learning to cope with life.

Moodiness is different from unhappiness in teenagers. Moodiness is usually an attitude that is part of a developmental phase during adolescence. But unhappiness is generally related to a personal situation that has caused difficulties or disappointment for the teenager. Learning to handle problems with girlfriends or boyfriends, issues that arise at school, or family problems can create periods of unhappiness.

The teenager's agenda concerning unhappiness is to talk with best friends but only when he or she feels ready. If parents try to probe, they generally meet denial, resistance, or a wall of silence. Remember, teenagers aren't always sure about what they feel. They're confused by the meaning and appropriateness of their feelings, so talking can seem almost impossible. If they have grown up with parents who helped them to talk about feelings and modeled this behavior themselves, it may be relatively easy for them and their parents to discuss feelings, including unhappiness.

The parent's agenda about the teenager's unhappiness is to worry a great deal, sometimes giving the teenager the feeling that there is something wrong with him or her. Again, it is important for parents to accept the normality of these feelings and their importance in teenage development. Teenagers need to learn to handle unhappy feelings, understand them, and know that they will get over them.

You can help your teen master these important skills in using the steps that follow.

FIRST STEP

Think about how observant you have been about your teenager's unhappy periods. What attitude have you adopted? Are you supportive and understanding or do you act annoyed and become critical?

SECOND STEP

You may have reacted critically to your teenager's unhappiness, with such comments as, "Why do you have such an unhappy face? It doesn't do any good to be so upset over your boyfriend, and frankly, he isn't worth it! Just concentrate on your studies and you won't have time to be so upset."

If you have reacted in this way, say, "I realize that sometimes I don't know what to say when you seem upset. I feel frustrated when you're unhappy and I can't help you, so I act annoyed. I don't think that's fair. I have to learn to be more understanding when you feel that way. I'll really try to be more tolerant, and I hope sometimes you will talk to me when you're feeling unhappy. If you don't want to talk, I'll understand."

THIRD STEP

Tell your teenager, "The thing that I notice is that you always seem to get over your unhappiness, so you must have found some way to get over those feelings, even though we don't talk about what's bothering you. I'm glad that you can do that. I have to accept that sometimes you'll have to struggle with your feelings, and I shouldn't worry so much because you're strong enough to handle them. I'll try not to worry so much." In this way you support your teenager's resourcefulness and express your confidence in his or her ability to handle her life.

FOURTH STEP

All teenagers experience unhappiness, but prolonged, intense unhappiness is not normal and may be an indication of depression. If your teenager's unhappiness persists and is not just periodic, then it is wise to get a professional consultation. In a later section of this book, I suggest ways that will help you talk to your teenager about getting professional help.

Taking Responsibility for Inappropriate Behavior

One of the great battles between teenagers and their parents is created by the clash between parental advice and the teenage need to be autonomous and independent. From years of grappling with the world, parents have actually discovered the best way to do some things, but teenagers will rarely admit this and so they routinely reject parental advice. Parents can also tell when the kid has made a mistake, but most teenagers would rather die than admit this.

Parents tend to become exasperated with their teenager's unwillingness to admit or take responsibility for their mistakes and poor judgment. They have endless dialogues in which they try to get the kid to admit to a poor attitude or bad judgment or even to having been unfair. They exhaust themselves trying to make their teenager see the light about behavior or attitudes. Usually they just end up verbally shoving their point of view down the kid's unwilling throat.

The more obvious the point is, the harder parents try, and the more frustrated they become. This leads to some amusing but very inappropriate behavior on the parents' part. Some parents go back to the FBI style of parenting to make their point, watching to catch the kid in the act. They hope that once they have the goods on him or her, they can prove that they are right. FBI parents accuse in a triumphant tone, "You see? You're doing it right now—teasing your sister."

Other parents overtalk this issue and trap themselves in endless, nonproductive dialogues. "What do you mean, you didn't have time to do your chores? How can you stand there and lie to me like that? The teenager would love to say, "It's easy!" but doesn't dare. So the parents are met by sullen silence and end up with a stalemate.

Parents need to understand that one of the most difficult aspects of maturing is admitting that you are wrong or taking responsibility for inappropriate behavior. But when you stop to think about it, how many adults do you know who can readily say, "I'm sorry. You are right and I was wrong"? How easily does your spouse, boss, or mother-in-law say, "I made a mistake. I should have done it your way"? These phrases do not flow easily from most adults, so why should we expect more from teenagers?

For many of us, admitting that we have made a mistake is one of the most formidable developmental tasks at any age, because it carries with it a feeling of humiliation or shame. When we admit that we were wrong, it feels like an admission of incompetence, and we fear that we will lose the respect of other people. That's why this difficult task of taking responsibility is rarely modeled by adults for teenagers to learn.

The teenager's agenda in denying mistakes is to preserve a sense of being grown-up while struggling with in many ways still being a little kid. When teenagers make mistakes, they realize that they are not as capable as they want to feel and that they still have things to learn. Admitting this to parents is very difficult because it threatens to cast teenagers back into the little-kid category, directly challenging their need for autonomy.

Like all of us, teenagers struggle to accept the fact that it feels bad to do something poorly, to be unsuccessful, to fail. This contradicts their grandiose feeling that they can do anything, and it causes conflict. This is only aggravated when parents try to force teenagers to admit their mistakes.

The parents' agenda is to get their teenager to admit responsibility, so they engage in relentless arguments to drive home their point, even if it kills both of them. In their frustration, they forget that even if on rare occasions they succeed and the kid says, "Okay, I screwed up," their victories won't really change their teenager's behavior, and their agressive attempts will usually harden the resistance. Your teenager may conclude, "You'll never admit that I'm right, so why should I admit that you are?"

Parents need to realize that they can't argue the teenager into admitting anything. Persisting only creates a contest of wills, and they can hold out as long as you can. In their attempts to resist your arguments, teenagers become more rigid and less willing or able to consider your opinion on any subject, just on general principle.

Parents need to have more empathy for their teenager's struggle to accept responsibility for his or her actions, and they need to stop trying to convince the kid that he or she is wrong.

FIRST STEP

Before discussing this issue with your teenager, observe your own behavior. How often do you admit your own mistakes out loud to other people? (Just saying, "God, was I dumb!" in the privacy of the shower doesn't count!) Do you ever admit to your teenager that you were wrong? Are you asking your teenager to do something difficult that you never model?

If you rarely admit your own mistakes, you need to begin by telling your teenager, "Look, I don't do this any better than you do. It's hard for me to admit when I'm wrong. I have to work on it, too." This will make your teenager much less defensive.

SECOND STEP

Tell your teenager, "I realize that many times I try to force you to admit that you've done something wrong or that my way would have been better. But I can see that the way I go about it is so annoying that you don't want to hear anything I have to say. It probably makes you feel more defensive. I realize that I may be as much a part of the problem as you are. From now on I'll try harder to let you have your own opinion, even if it's different from mine."

This is a good thing to say even if you don't think that your attitude is a factor, because it makes the kid feel that other people can be wrong, too.

THIRD STEP

In a quiet moment tell your teenager, "I know that it's really difficult for people, including adults, to admit that they're wrong or that they could have found a better way to do something. I know that's hard for me to do, and I think it's hard for you. Do you think that you could try not to be so defensive when I question your opinion or decisions? Maybe sometimes you could admit that you haven't acted responsibly? I think you will feel better if you discover that admitting you've made a mistake doesn't mean anything bad about you. I don't think it does."

FOURTH STEP

If your teenager isn't willing to change the pattern and take responsibility for inappropriate actions, don't argue because it won't help.

Just accept the fact that he or she isn't ready to deal with this issue now. But that doesn't mean the kid will grow up to be a criminal or con artist just because he can't admit his mistakes. This developmental task is just taking a little longer. It takes assurance, maturity, and confidence to accept the less attractive aspects of ourselves and still feel that we are good persons, worthy of respect and love.

Say, "I'm not going to argue or try to convince you that you are wrong anymore. I hope that someday you will learn to be able to admit your mistakes. It's a great characteristic to have when you grow up. You are a terrific kid, and other people will respect you for your willingness to admit your mistakes and be responsible." This makes plain that you still value this goal and you believe it's one he or she will eventually develop.

6

SEXUAL BEHAVIOR

"Don't grow up—please!"

Sexual Issues and Your Teenager

Even after the so-called sexual revolution, many parents find that they are very uneasy with the notion of their children becoming sexually aware and active. Liberal attitudes do nothing to quell the anxiety that arises when they realize that teenage sexuality can no longer be ignored. So, in the privacy of their bedrooms, they have dialogues like this:

>"I think it's time for you to tell him."
>"Tell him what?"
>"You know! Sex!"
>"Why me?"
>"Because you're the father."
>"Well, how much does he know?"
>"Probably more than we do."
>"So why am I talking to him? Besides, don't they learn that stuff at school or on TV?"
>"Yes, but don't you think we should teach him something?"
>"What?"

As you can see, this subject creates considerable anxiety and ambivalence for many parents. When it comes time to discuss sex with their teenagers, parents are in agony. "I can't stand the idea that my teenager is interested in this stuff. It makes me feel so old! Why did they ever have to grow up? I'm not ready for this. I never learned to talk about my own sexuality! How can I talk about theirs? I just want to say, "Don't do it!"

Teenagers usually begin to tune in on their parents' anxiety. "They're acting so weird. They must be getting ready to tell me about sex. This is going to be really awful!"

When the parent finally gets up the nerve to say, "I want to talk to you about something," the teenager is ready. "Did I do something wrong? "No, no," protests the parent. "It's about sex." The kid has a snappy answer prepared. "What do you want to know?" The reluctant parent recognizes an out and concedes, "Okay, that takes care of it!"

In the past, parents avoided this subject altogether, and their teenagers learned about sex through experience and from their peers. Not the best way, but the most common because even concerned parents lacked a comfortable way to talk about sex.

Most parents never learned about sex from their own parents. If sex was discussed, it was done formally and rather awkwardly, in a single session, rather than as a natural topic of discussion throughout childhood.

So sex has always been difficult for most parents to discuss with their children, but now in the age of AIDS, the subject is much more worrisome and creates a great deal of anxiety and confusion for parents and teens. But parents can no longer allow their discomfort to prevent them from discussing sex with their children, because ignorance about sexual practices can be life threatening.

From this time on, parents need to be involved in educating themselves and their children about both the beauty and danger of sex. There is no longer any question that parents must talk about sex and contraception, which means that the job of parenting has become even more demanding.

Parents' values about sex are frequently very different from those of their teenagers, and many adults become even more conservative in their views when it comes to their teenager's sexuality. While current health issues may encourage more conservative sexual behavior in general, there will always be some major conflicts over the teens' need to explore their sexuality and the parents' struggle to accept this as inevitable.

This section cannot cover all the issues related to sexually transmitted diseases, pregnancy, and contraception, but it will discuss ways to communicate with your teenager to create positive dialogues concerning these and other sexual issues.

Opening Up a Dialogue about Sex

We have already touched on how difficult it is for parents to talk about sex with their teenagers. It may take several tries to get a dialogue going, and you may always feel some discomfort. Keeping that in mind, let's give these new approaches a sincere effort.

FIRST STEP

In order to talk with confidence and comfort to your teenager about sexual issues, it is extremely important that you become more knowledgeable about sexuality in teenagers and particularly about sexually transmitted diseases. You must be well informed if you are to be convincing with your teenager. Please consult the For Further Reading section for books and resources to assist you in learning more about these very important issues.

SECOND STEP

You can begin to open up a dialogue about sexual issues in the following way: Say to your teenager, "I think it's time we learned to be more comfortable discussing subjects like sex with each other. I don't mean you have to tell me everything that you are doing or thinking. But there may be ways in which I could be helpful to you if you have questions or feelings that concern you. It's really too bad that this is so awkward for me, and I'm not sure about the best way for the two of us to talk. But let's just try it so that we can make it a more comfortable topic.

"When I was growing up, we just never talked about sex in our family." If you did discuss sex in your family, and you still feel awkward, you can say, "Even though my parents were really open about talking about sex, it's different when it's your own kids, and it really is more difficult than I would have thought." This helps your teenager feel that the problem is yours, and this creates less resistance to the subject.

THIRD STEP

Tell your teenager, "I know it's easier for you to talk to your friends about sex, and I am not criticizing you for that. I remember that I felt that way, too. But I would hate to think that you're only learning about sex through your friends. Maybe we can go to some lectures together or just get information and share it with each other. I hope you don't think this is a dumb idea, but if it feels too uncomfortable to you, I will accept that. I need to learn more about the sexual issues that affect you. I also think that some of my experiences and ideas about sex might be very helpful to you." Of course, say this only if it is true.

FOURTH STEP

If the dialogue between you and your teenager is going to work, you will need to learn to be more accepting about your teenager's values concerning sex, even if they are different from yours. For example, some teenagers think that it's all right to have intercourse if they really care about someone, but most parents don't.

If you are dealing with this particular difference in values, you might say in a noncritical tone, "I don't feel that way, but I'm not judging you. I hope we can discuss our differences about this. I'll be honest with you. I wish that I had more control over this issue, like when you were a little kid and I could say, 'Don't do it or I'll send you to your room.' But all I can do is tell you that sexual intercourse is more complicated than just having sex. I'm not sure that you want to hear this, but I really hope that you will learn that sex takes a lot more maturity than most teenagers possess. I can't change the way you feel about this, but I hope we can continue to talk."

By talking in this way, you create the possibility of ongoing communication, which is the only way you have a chance to influence your teenager. Say, "I worry more about this issue because of the risk of pregnancy and sexually transmitted diseases. I really hope that you are informed about these things and care enough about yourself to be cautious."

This type of dialogue should only go on as long as the teenager seems willing to listen. If you encounter a lot of resistance you may have to take these steps one at a time and continue the discussion whenever the opportunity presents itself.

FIFTH STEP

Sharing your own experiences of learning about sex can help build a feeling of understanding between you and your teenager. Tell her, "I was thinking about what I learned about sex when I was growing up." Either share some of the helpful things that you learned or explain that you didn't learn much of anything from your parents. Discuss how these experiences affected your attitude toward your own sexuality as an adult. For example, "My parents talked to me about sex in a very practical way, and I would like to share the things that I found helpful." If your teenager says that he or she already knows that stuff, just say, "I'm glad."

If your parents didn't teach you much about sexual issues, say, "I really didn't get any help from my parents about this. I had to learn on my own and it wasn't always the best way, so I felt confused sometimes. Maybe I can tell you some of the things that I didn't know and see if it's helpful to you. If you already know what I'm telling you, just stop me." This type of approach encourages your teenager to understand you better and makes it possible for him or her to ask any questions.

SIXTH STEP

You need to learn that while your knowledge about sex is important, the most important thing to your teenager is your attitude toward the issue. If your teenager learns that he or she can talk to you, and that you will even admit that you don't know everything, you will become more comfortable together, and he or she will respect your honesty.

Tell your teenager, "I hope you can believe that no matter what issue comes up about sex, I will really try to understand your point of view, even if I don't agree with you. That's because I love you and want to help you solve whatever problem might occur.

"Since we are talking about this, I want you to know that if you ever had a serious problem, like pregnancy, I would really try to be understanding and help you. I don't want you to think I'm condoning getting pregnant, but my first concern would be to help you. The saddest thing I can imagine is a teenager who couldn't tell her parents about something like that and had to handle it without help."

Parents have to learn that the most important thing they can do in this area is to create an atmosphere of understanding and education. Face the fact that you have very little control over your teenager's sexual behavior, but you can have great influence in helping him think about and understand sexual issues and his feelings about sex. Real control comes from the open dialogue that exists between you and your teenager.

Teenagers in Love

Social development is a major concern for some parents, even when their kids are small. Many parents encourage their kids to be social and outgoing at a very early age, as seen in the endless round of birthday parties and sleepovers that some children attend. They worry that their youngsters will miss important experiences if they are not socially involved. Their concerns about their teenagers' social development include the fear that they will be boy or girl crazy when they're too young, or that they will never develop an interest in the opposite sex.

So when teenagers begin to have close friends of both sexes, parents feel that they are being appropriately social. This sense of relief usually lasts until their child—now thirteen, fourteen, or fifteen—starts acting weird, spaced out, and dreamy. They know it's not drugs because it only happens after the teenager has been talking to a particular boy or girl. Parents are treated to endless conversations in which a particular boy or girl is described in glowing terms—strong signs that the kid is in love!

Parents think it's cute when young children get crushes, but they panic at the first scent of teenage love in bloom. They have long talks with spouses and friends, in which they hatch plots to break up the romance, including finding a better job for the boyfriend's father in another city—perhaps Moscow. Or they parade lots of attractive guys through the house hoping that fickleness will win the day! All of this panic results from the adults' fear that their teenager is about to form a lifelong relationship with an inappropriate person.

How inappropriate? Let's listen to some of the comments I hear when parents express their feelings about the object of their teenager's affection. "My kid says she's in love with the most wonderful guy, who just happens to look like a cross between a zombie and a biker. This guy walks into my house with his head down, grunts hello, and can't put more than five words together. Then my daughter says, 'Isn't he great?' I want to throw up! Where did we go wrong?"

Parents are often very uncomfortable with the level of devotion that teenagers express when they're in love. "Watching these kids drives me crazy. You'd think their bodies were glued together. Her boyfriend can't say five words to me, but they talk on the phone for hours. My phone! If this kid ever became part of the family, I could never face my mother!"

If this seems exaggerated, you should talk to some of the parents who come to see me because of this issue. I have heard parents propose some of the most humorous plans to get their teenagers to see the person they love more "realistically." (This means seeing him the way their parents do and dumping the turkey.) One mother asked her daughter if she ever noticed how often other boys stare at her and seem interested in dating her. Another mother tried this. "Gee, wouldn't it be fun to date Bob Thompson? He seems like such a neat kid." The smart teenager turned to her mother and said, "Why don't you go out with him if you think he's so great?"

In other words, you can't talk kids out of their feelings and attitudes, but you can comfort yourself with the knowledge that "falling in love," even inappropriately, is another stage that teenagers must go through as they are growing up.

Another source of anxiety for parents centers around the sexual behavior that inevitably develops as the teenagers become more involved with each other. Some parents handle their anxiety by actively discouraging physical contact. When they see their teenagers in sexually suggestive positions—hugging, kissing, or sitting close together—they nail them with a laser-beam look! This is a cold stare that threatens to drill a hole through their heads if they so much as move toward each other. When teenagers get caught in a situation like this, they do what I call the "quick-jump-straighten-up" move. In a single gesture it says, "We didn't do nothin'!"

In an attempt to find out how serious the situation is, some parents resort to private investigation or spying techniques. They look for evidence in letters, telephone calls, or by listening through the walls of their teenager's room. The parents' agenda is to prevent their kid from getting overly serious about this love stuff. They desperately want to have control over something that they really can't control, and it's very frustrating.

The teenager's agenda is to experience and explore this feeling of being in love with all its complicated ups and downs. Remember, teenagers learn a great deal about relationships when they go through these experiences. When parents learn to talk effectively about being in love, they can be extremely helpful to their teenagers in sorting out these complicated emotions. So give it a try!

FIRST STEP

Begin by observing your attitude and the way your react when your teenager falls in love. One of the main issues for your teenager is to avoid feeling foolish or making an obvious mistake, particularly in the choice of a boy- or girlfriend. If your attitude is openly negative, your teenager is liable to cling even more tightly to the object of his or her affection because sticking with the relationship and making it work, even if it's inappropriate, will be a way of proving that you're wrong.

SECOND STEP

Tell your teenager in a supportive tone, "I can see that you really like James a lot. That must feel great." If you have expressed negative feelings about your teenager's relationship, say, "I'm sorry that I haven't been more enthusiastic about your relationship with Jody. I want you to know that it's difficult for a parent when a little kid grows up so fast. Seeing you fall in love for the first time is not easy. What you're doing isn't wrong in any way. It's just something that will take time for us to get used to.

"I remember that I had some of those feelings when I was younger. They can be wonderful sometimes, and other times it's really painful. I guess I feel protective toward you because I don't want you to get hurt. But I realize you should be able to have this experience and go through it your own way. I will really try not to say things that make you feel uncomfortable about your boy [girl] friend.

THIRD STEP

Tell your teenager, "I realize that you really have strong feelings about James [Jody]. I am not trying to say that you're not in love or that your relationship isn't important. But it takes a long time to learn about love. The feelings are wonderful yet confusing, so at times you may feel mixed up. I'm only telling you this because if you ever feel confused about your feelings, maybe we can talk. I would really like to help you if you need me. If you don't want to talk, that's okay, too. I could have used someone to talk to when I was your age. I'm only telling you this because I love you very much."

If you have a teenager who is in a painful, unhappy love relationship and doesn't seem to be able to get out of it, you should
consider having him or her talk to a professional. Refer to the section
on preparing your teenager for accepting professional help.

As you think about the issues in this section, try to imagine how
it would have felt for one of your parents to have been this understanding when you were growing up. If your teenager asks, "Why are you
acting this way? You never talk to me like this." You should reply,
"Well, I have a lot to learn, and I am trying to become much more
understanding about things that are important to you. I want you to
know that it feels a lot better to talk to you like this than the way I did
in the past."

Finding Teenagers in Amorous Situations

When parents find their teenagers in amorous situations, hugging and
kissing passionately, they experience surprise, resentment, and discomfort. Even the most liberal parent occasionally thinks, If I hear
one more psychologist say that sexual exploration is a normal part of
teenage development, I'll scream! I'd like to see one of those smart-ass
professionals deal calmly with teenagers who cling to each other as if
their lives depended on it.

What most parents want to say is something powerful and au-
thoritative that will cool the fires of young love. Something like, "If I
ever find you two like this again, I'll personally ship you to the planet
No Sex and you won't see each other for centuries!" This threat
probably won't dampen your teenager's passion, but it may help you
feel that you are in control for a moment. However, a moment of
control is nothing in the face of all those hormones!

The goal in this situation is to let the teenagers know that you
understand the normalcy of their behavior and are prepared to be
reasonable, yet you expect them to show better control than they have
in the past. Remember, you only have a limited amount of control
over this situation. You don't want your teenager to feel that sexuality
must be hidden, but he or she must learn when, how, and where it is
appropriate to express these feelings.

FIRST STEP

Occasionally you may find your teenager in an amorous situation with
a boyfriend. I am not referring to a momentary kiss or hug, which is

normal and healthy. I mean embracing on a bed or couch, which creates the potential for greater sexual involvement.

If you have followed the previously suggested procedures for opening up a dialogue about sex, you have already established a more comfortable environment for addressing this issue. When you are confronted by passionate behavior that makes you uncomfortable, you may be able to handle the situation in a way that shows understanding for your teenager's behavior and establishes appropriate standards.

SECOND STEP

When you find your teenager "making out" with his or her girl- or boyfriend on the couch or on a bed, try to say with a firm, light tone, "I know that you really like each other but I'm not comfortable when you don't show good self-control in front of the family. I realize that you feel sexually attracted to each other, but I hope that you will use good judgment about your sexual attraction. I'm not going to lecture you about this, and my purpose is not to embarrass you. But you need to understand that expressing your strong sexual feelings lying on the couch or on the bed is unacceptable. I understand that your feelings are normal, but you may not express yourself that way here."

If you are able to respond in a matter-of-fact, accepting way to sexual behavior, it will not become a huge issue, and your teenager will experience your view in a positive way. In particular, your openness about sexuality not only normalizes it and shows that you accept him or her as a sexual being but also establishes that you have expectations about how she should express these feelings.

Once you have confronted this behavior, you will probably not have to deal with it over and over. Teenagers would rather avoid the embarrassment and so become more careful and restrained when they are around the family.

THIRD STEP

If you have a teenager who persists in acting out sexually, this is the next step. In a tone that conveys firmness but not anger, say, "I can see that no matter what I say you and your boy [girl] friend don't want to control your sexual feelings as I have asked. I know how strong these feelings can be, but you have to show more control and respect my rules in our house. If you can figure out a way to handle yourselves so that it doesn't happen again in this house, I won't say anything else. But if you can't solve this problem, I will limit the time that your boy-[girl] friend can spend here and talk to him [her]. I'll only do this if you don't comply with my expectations."

As you may have noticed, the emphasis is on control without judgment. The expectations are clear without making the teenagers feel guilty for their behavior. Guilt rarely controls the expression of sexual feelings.

Finding Your Teenager's Contraceptive Devices

When parents discover or even suspect that their teenagers have contraceptive devices, they may cringe and wonder why children ever have to grow up. Even responsible, enlightened parents flinch at the sight of condoms in a drawer that used to hold a first-class collection of baseball cards! Many parents have said to me, "I know safe sex is an important issue, but I still hate condom ads on television because I don't like to think about how anxious my teenager's sexuality makes me."

These feelings are understandable because finding contraceptive devices confirms the reality that your teenager is contemplating or has already had a sexual relationship. Try not to say the first thing that springs to your lips, like, "Where did you get these?" or "I'll kill him! What if you get pregnant?"

There are many other remarks that are probably used to scare some sense into teenagers. Among the classics are, "Will he take care of you?" "What about the baby?" "What about school?" "Are you ready to support her if you get her pregnant?" "What about sexual diseases?" Parents say all these things out of panic and worry, but these statements just force teenagers to go underground with their feelings and values.

If you haven't had to face this situation, I hope that the next section will help you express your feelings in a way that may have a positive influence on your teenager.

Remember, that's all you can do! You can't lock your teenager up until he or she is an adult, even though that thought may have crossed your mind. Some of you might be thinking that if we can stop kids from drinking, we can keep them from having sex. Maybe what's needed is a good, strong law and an army of people to enforce it!

That's how uncomfortable some parents are with the notion that their teenagers are sexually active. Let's see if we can continue to understand and accept teenage sexuality as a normal growth pattern, yet find ways to exert a positive influence on their behavior and sense of responsibility.

FIRST STEP

Tell your teenager in a firm, supportive tone, "I need to tell you something that concerns me. I found your condoms [or diaphragm or pills]." Your teenager may feel that you have violated his or her privacy. "You couldn't have found them without going through my drawers. Can't I have any privacy?"

Say, "I apologize if I intruded. You're not in trouble with me. I'm not mad, but I am concerned about how careful you are being sexually. I realize that maybe you just want to have them in case you get involved sexually. I really hope you will use good judgment. I want to understand your views about contraception, and I need you to understand mine. I promise I won't preach to you about morals."

Most teenagers won't have a clear explanation of their behavior, so don't expect one. Sometimes when they buy contraceptives, they are acknowledging their sexual and emotional desires and have decided to use protection. Other teens are simply fantasizing about being prepared when their imaginary sexual encounter finally occurs.

Of course, your response will depend on your values, but my opinion is that you should say, "I will always love you and care about you whatever you choose to do. But I have to tell you that I wish you would wait until you are older and have more experience in life. Then you will be able to make better decisions about when and with whom you want to have sex. Think about it, and if you want to talk about it more, I would really like to help you with this." (The more conservative may want to say, "when you get married," and continue the dialogue from that perspective.)

I realize that this may be repetitious, but I can't overemphasize the importance of this type of communication in having a positive influence on your teenager. Letting your teenager know how understanding you are prepared to be creates a tremendous feeling of security about your relationship. Although the teenager may not say it out loud, a likely reaction is, If we can talk about this stuff, we can talk about anything! This sense of acceptance by parents promotes respect for their ideas and a willingness to listen.

7

LOOSE ENDS

"I thought I was finished!"

Allowance and Money

Money and its uses—finally a topic that's equally interesting to adults and teens! The issue of allowance and spending money for teenagers is not likely to create massive amounts of anxiety for parents, but like many other issues, it can seem like a big, big deal to teenagers. Contemporary teenagers have so many social opportunities and personal reasons for spending money that financing them can require the services of a full-time accountant.

Parents are often seen as the nearest branch of the United States Treasury or, better yet, an automatic teller machine. Some teenagers feel that all they have to do is submit a request and the amount will be delivered. Meanwhile, you see your vacation and retirement funds supporting every clothing merchant in the country! Teenagers tend to complain about never having enough money, while you try to explain your financial situation, complete with graphs and bank statements. Talk about different agendas!

Parents tend to get involved in this issue by telling their teenagers about how they had to work for everything they got. "You kids don't know how easy you have it!" Since teenagers tune out this story in less than two seconds, let's look at the value of an allowance and how you can use it to teach your teenager something about responsibility.

Some parents avoid the topic of allowances entirely by simply giving their teenager money whenever the need arises, but then they tend to complain about how it is spent. Other parents who are financially secure just don't think about the money, giving it freely without any consideration for what their teenager is learning about handling money. An allowance is a way to teach your teenager about the value of money, which will be essential when he or she is an adult and living independently.

FIRST STEP

If you are able to afford it, ask for your teenager's thoughts on what is an appropriate allowance. Unless these expectations are very unrealistic compared to your financial situation, it's better to let him or her take responsibility for suggesting a fair amount for his allowance.

SECOND STEP

Once you have agreed on the amount of the allowance, tell your teenager, "Remember, this is your money to use in whatever way you choose, but if you spend it all in one day, you'll have to find a way to get along without money until next week." This helps the kid learn to be responsible for budgeting and handling financial situations.

THIRD STEP

If the allowance includes money for such things as lunch, transportation, and personal necessities, this should be spelled out very specifically. For example, you might tell your teenager, "Your allowance includes money for lunch each day. If you spend it on other things and end up with no money on Friday, you'll have to make your lunch at home or think of some other solution." If on Friday you hear complaints that you're just being mean, don't give in on this issue, feeling that you are depriving your teenager. He or she needs to learn the importance of handling money.

FOURTH STEP

You can help your teenager to have more options and learn about earning by making the following proposal: "If you need more money and you let me know that you want to earn some, we can negotiate some chores that you can do to earn extra money. If you don't want to do that, it's your choice, but then you will have to stay within your allowance. I just don't think that extra money should be free." Be sure that these chores are really work so that your teenager learns that money doesn't come easily. Say, "I'm not doing this to be hard on you, but it's really important that you learn to control your spending or take responsibility for earning more money."

If you can't afford to give your teenager extra money, even for doing extra chores, you need to explain that the allowance is based on family income and that's all you can afford. If your teenager needs more, getting a job is a possibility to consider, but you're not saying that he or she has to do that.

FIFTH STEP

If your teenager seems to have difficulty planning for expenses and continually comes to you to be bailed out, you need to put some limits on the situation. Tell your teenager in a calm manner, "You seem to spend all your money on records and clothes and then complain to me that you don't have enough. If I'm wrong and you can explain the difficulty to me, I'd be glad to work on this problem with you. I really don't want you to have difficulty handling money when you get older, so I would like to help you with this now." If your teenager doesn't want your help, you will have to accept that this lesson will be learned later on.

Instead of complaining to your teenager about how much he or she spends and yet continuing to supply money on demand, limit the amount of allowance and spending money with a very clear approach. When you do this you are teaching the reality that parents don't or can't always magically take care of problems, monetary and otherwise.

Getting a Job

This issue is closely related to negotiating about allowance because it concerns your teenager's need to earn money and learn about life and financial responsibility. Usually teenagers decide to get a job because they want a new car, a trip, new clothes, or a college education. Once in a while, teenagers shock their parents by deciding to work just to be more independent and relieve their parents of economic burdens. (These teenagers are exceptions, but they do exist outside the pages of books!)

Many teenagers don't give the idea of work serious thought because they don't see any need for it. Mom and Dad are generous, and there are so many more interesting things to do than go to work. They see a lifetime of work ahead of them and are reluctant to give up the leisure that many of them enjoy. They are also legitimately involved in schoolwork and extracurricular activities that make working an impractical notion. However, most teenagers can mature and grow emotionally by having a job on weekends, during vacation, or for a limited time after school.

FIRST STEP

Think about your attitude toward your teenager and work. Consider realistically if he or she is organized and resourceful enough to be able to handle a job in addition to his or her other responsibilities. If you think it is a reasonable idea, negotiate.

SECOND STEP

If your teenager wants to work, say that you respect the desire to work, acknowledging that it is a responsible, mature idea. Ask how your teenager plans to work and handle all his or her other commitments. Help him or her to be sure that the planning has been thorough, without sounding as if you are challenging his or her good sense. If the idea seems reasonable, consider giving your go-ahead about having a job—with some ground rules.

Say, "You seem to have thought the situation through clearly, so I will let you try working for one semester. If your grades stay up and you can still take care of your other responsibilities, you can keep your job. If problems develop, you'll have to drop some activities, and that may include working."

THIRD STEP

If your teenager hasn't thought this issue through clearly but still wants to try working, don't say, "You don't know what you're doing!" Negotiate a plan that is acceptable to you and is agreeable to your teen. For example, "You can try working for one semester. If you keep your grades up and can take care of your other responsibilities, then you can keep your job. If working causes problems and you neglect the other areas of your life, you'll have to decide which activity to drop. I'm not saying you aren't capable of handling all this. We'll just have to see how it goes."

FOURTH STEP

If you have a teenager who hasn't shown a great deal of responsibility toward school and other obligations but wants to get a job, don't immediately be discouraging by saying, "How in the world could you handle a job when you can't even manage to do your homework and the few chores you have around here?"

Consider saying in an interested tone, "What makes you feel that you can handle this job?" Your teenager may reply that it's different from school because it's something that he or she really wants to do. This is the time to negotiate: "I need you to try harder in school, so what kind of agreement can we make if we let you get a job?" If your teenager says, "I will keep my grades up and do what you ask at home," you can plan to evaluate after a month. If he or she doesn't say something like this, suggest at least passing grades or a good effort indicated by the teachers' evaluations.

Say, "We will let you get a job and keep it as long as you're responsible." You must be fair on this point. If there is some improvement in grades and in cooperation at home, tell your teenager that keeping the job is acceptable, but you still want to see an improvement and continued effort.

Remember that there are some teenagers who begin to learn responsibility by working because it helps to build their self-esteem. So you can use this approach to motivate your teenager to improve in some of the areas that concern you.

FIFTH STEP

If you have a teenager who fails in the effort to hold a job and keep up with other responsibilities, say, "I'm sorry that this didn't work out for you, but you can't work the next semester. If you want to try again, depending on how you do in school and at home, I really want to give you another chance. I don't want you to get discouraged." Of course, this approach is not realistic if your teenager has to work for economic

166

reasons. Then work can't be linked to your teenager's performance in school.

Grades

Parents tend to drive their teenager crazy asking about, checking on, and worrying about grades because poor grades are much more upsetting to parents than they are to the kids. Many teenagers tend to live so much in the present—or even for the moment—that they can't see the relationship between studying chemistry today and succeeding in the future.

Other teenagers act as if they don't worry about grades, but they really are concerned, and this attitude only increases their parents' exasperation. Some parents feel very anxious because they think that grades are an indication of what kind of future their kid is going to have.

This issue creates heated exchanges that only widen the gap between puzzled students and their frantic parents. "You'd better get those grades up! You'll never get into a good college if they get a look at your last report card. You're not living up to your potential. Maybe if you spent less time on the telephone you'd make the dean's list again."

Teenagers frequently respond nonverbally to these remarks with looks of bewilderment, sighs, and rolling their eyes. They're thinking, If they don't get off my back, I'll just fail and get it over with. They act like it's the end of the world if I don't keep a B average. What's so important about chemistry, anyway?"

It may help you to realize that many teenagers who struggle with academics in high school do very well in college when they have matured a bit. So life isn't over for teens who have difficulty with grades and studies in high school.

Parents tend to react emotionally to their teenager's grades. If they suspect or find out that their teenager is getting poor grades, they may say in the heat of the moment, "You'd better get those grades up if you want to get a car! I expect nothing lower than a B." If your teenager has always had to struggle for good grades, it's simply unrealistic to state such expectations.

If a teenager has always had good grades and suddenly falls down, parents tend to say, "How could you let this happen? You'd better not let this happen again! I'm really disappointed in you!" Statements like these rarely improve grades, but they do prevent you from having a positive influence on your teenager's attitude toward school and the future.

I realize that many parents may be wondering if I am suggesting that they stand quietly by and watch their children fail. Absolutely not! I don't think you should remain passive in the face of failure, but you do need to be realistic about how much influence you can have on your teenager's grades. Parents need to learn that grades don't always tell the future. Many kids who just have average grades become very successful later in life. I hope the following section will help you grapple with this troublesome issue.

FIRST STEP

As a good, observing parent, ask yourself how often you talk to your teenager's teacher if you are really concerned about grades. Do you communicate regularly or only when there is a problem? Do you discuss grades in an annoyed tone of voice? Are you a parent who is always telling your teenager that he or she can do better without finding out if the kid feels that he or she is already doing his or her best.

SECOND STEP

Instead of focusing on specific grades, focus more on your teenager's efforts and responsibility toward school. Telling your teenager what grades to get creates unnecessary pressure, and he or she may be unable to live up to your specific expectations, even with a tremendous effort.

Many teenagers are not mature enough to predict accurately how they will do in school. For example, many teenagers say at the beginning of the semester that they will get all B's that year. Parents cheer them on. The kids pump themselves up because they have a fresh start and don't realize that it will take hard work as well as adrenaline to get him through the year. Parents are sometimes as unrealistic as their teenager and may be temporarily relieved by these predictions of success.

THIRD STEP

If you have a teenager who is a good student and has a bad semester, but you have confidence in his or her ability to recover, try to say this in a concerned positive tone: "You usually do so well. What do you think happened this semester?" If he can't come up with a clear answer, say "I guess its hard to figure out how you let this semester get away from you."

If he or she comes up with a good explanation, say, "I can see that you really understand the problem that you had this semester. I know that you're very capable and you won't let it continue." Another helpful comment is, "I really understand that you feel badly about your grades falling, but you're so capable that you will get them back up."

Some parents may be saying, "This guy has to be kidding! If that kid lets this happen again, he [she] will be locked in his [her] room until the grades improve!" What I am telling you is that most kids who usually have good grades bounce back from a bad semester because they don't like having poor grades. You need to learn to trust them. If your teenager receives this kind of understanding, it will be more motivating than all nine thousand lectures you have prepared!

FOURTH STEP

If you have a teenager who has struggled in school and has a bad semester, some of the comments I suggested above will be helpful, but they should be slanted in this way. (We are talking here about the kind of teenager whom parents nag a lot about grades.) You should say, "I am really going to try not to react to the grades you got this semester. Instead, I want to figure out what we can do. I think we need to talk together with your teachers, not as a punishment but to improve the situation. We're going to set up a program until your grades improve."

FIFTH STEP

At the beginning of the new semester or anytime during the year when the problem of grades comes up, set up a procedure for your teenager to get a note from each teacher at the end of the month, indicating if he or she has a passing grade. If the grades are failing, insist that your teenager increase his or her study time until the grades improve.

If your teenager fails to get the teachers' notes, accept no excuses. Set a consequence until it is taken care of. Check with the teachers yourself to show your concern. Tell your teenager, "I would rather not have to go through this, but your grades are very important. If you get all passing grades we won't have to do this again."

SIXTH STEP

If you have a teenager who has a pattern of very poor grades, special evaluation is needed to see if there is a problem other than effort or attitude. There could be a learning disability that has been over-looked, or poor performance may be due to an emotional problem. Continued poor grades may indicate that the solution is not as simple as your teenager trying harder.

Teenage Dress

The style of dress that teenagers invent or adopt continues to mystify parents in every generation. Teenagers waltz out of the house fes-tooned in garish colors, mismatched patterns, and articles that wouldn't even be accepted by the Goodwill, the Salvation Army, or a thrift shop. Their outfits seem to defy all the conventions of good taste and even border on the indecent.

Parents wonder if this shabby dress is a subtle way of lobbying for a larger allowance. What will the neighbors think? Or is that "cos-tume" an announcement that your teenager has dropped college plans and is headed for the stage? What looks chic to the teenager seems ridiculous or even embarrassing to parents, who respond with remarks like, "You're not going out like that! You've been wearing that outfit for three weeks! What happened to the good clothes I bought you?"

In recent decades parents have endured the sight of their kids disguised in the leather "greaser" look, the hippie look, a sea of denim for every occasion, jeans that provide better ventilation than a screen door, and then back to leather in the recent "punk" style of clothing. Each style seemed to cause more despair than the one before it. Why do they want to make themselves look so ugly?

The teenager's agenda, when he or she stands before the mirror, is to be different, even unique, yet similar to every other teenager—to be noticed but not to be embarrassed. Clothes are a major part of the teenager's identity because they provide a way to be different from parents but accepted and comfortable in a peer group.

The parents' agenda is to impress their teenagers with the fact that people with green hair rarely get meaningful jobs. They pray that their kid will give up his earring and filthy Levi's, but taunting and criticizing are rarely effective techniques for changing clothing trends. So what does a parent do?

FIRST STEP

Try to remember that the same outrageously clad teenagers that you see everywhere will probably dress like every other adult, even their parents, once they mature. It's a developmental issue. The teenagers' agenda is that when they have to grow up they will accept the values of the adult world, including appropriate dress. But for now, forget it!

SECOND STEP

The next time you find yourself scrutinizing your teenager's outfit, take a quick look at your own behavior. Are you giving your teenager negative looks or making critical remarks about his or her attire? This will only guarantee the popularity of the outfit. If Mom or Dad hates it, it must be hot!

If you find yourself doing this, you need to tell your teenager, "I'm sorry for the comments I have made about the way you dress. As usual, I tend to forget what it was like when I was your age, and how important my clothes were to me. I really will try to be more tolerant about the way you choose to dress."

THIRD STEP

Tell your teenager, "I hope you will be understanding if I occasionally ask you to dress differently. I may suggest different clothing for a few events that are important for me, but it won't be that often."

This attitude helps your teenager feel accepted and be more receptive to your requests.

Conversations with Teenagers

Parents often look forward to the day when they can have truly interesting conversations with a kid who is finally old enough to tackle adult topics. You'll be able to stop discussing Cub Scouts and playground incidents and argue about politics. Parents even fantasize that their kids will be interested in them as people. With a few exceptions, it's a great fantasy.

The reality is that many parents find that having a conversation with their teenager is almost impossible. Teens who once talked to their parents with interest and enthusiasm suddenly confine their responses to throaty grunts similar to those produced by a hog! The same kid who conducts animated conversations with friends and ties up the phone for hours seems to have a one-word limit when talking to people over the age of thirty. Typical exchanges go like this.

> "How are things going at school?"
> "Okay."
> "Do you want dinner?"
> "Nope."
> "How's your girlfriend?"
> "All right."
> "What did you do with your friends?"
> "Nothing."

Some parents learn to communicate in short bursts, capitalizing on the notoriously short attention span that teenagers have for anything but their current obsessions. Parents who insist on conversing with their teenagers or try to expand two or three sentences into a dialogue often find themselves staring into a pair of glassy eyes. The slack jaw and spaced-out expression announce the teenager's boredom. You may be holding the body captive, but the mind has quietly escaped!

Other parents make the fatal mistake of trying to elicit conversation from their teenagers by "speaking their language"—using slang and popular phrases in an effort to be accepted and understood. Big mistake! This will usually earn them a look of disgust or a verbal rebuke. "God, Mom, you're so weird. Nobody talks like that!" Another wonderful conversation shot down.

The situation is not hopeless. You don't have to wait until your kid is twenty-one to have a meaningful conversation. But you will need to change the way you approach conversations, beginning with avoiding questions such as, "What did you do at school today?" "How are things going?" "Do you want to tell me anything?" These questions get just what you deserve, the famous yep, nope, I-don't-know answers.

Parents need to learn to enter the teenager's world not through slang, imitation, or intrusion, but by becoming aware of the things that are important to him or her. This can lead to many interesting and meaningful conversations.

FIRST STEP

Listen to yourself when you talk to your teenager. Do you ask the same general questions, which show no real interest in his or her life? "How was school?" is a classic in this category. Meaningful questions are personal and detailed enough to require more than a simple yes or no answer.

You also need to notice if you usually initiate conversations with your teenager for the sole purpose of discussing a problem. Teenagers catch on to this pattern quickly and become suspicious and uneasy when a conversation begins: "She's just trying to nail me, so the less I say the better."

Try to notice how often you talk to your teenager just for the sake of having a friendly, enjoyable conversation.

SECOND STEP

In order to become more sensitive to what your teenager feels is important, you will need to become a better observer. This means listening closely to what your teenager talks about with you and with friends, rather than just listening for potential problems.

What worries them? What interests do they share with friends? What problems do they have at school? What social issues seem to be recurring themes in their conversations? Can you name your teenager's favorite music groups? Why do they like certain films so much? These are just a few questions to guide your observation of your teenager's world so that you can have more relevant conversations.

THIRD STEP

How well do you understand your teenager's feelings? What hurts his or her feelings or makes him or her depressed? What causes happiness or produces anxiety? Awareness of these feelings can lead to some meaningful conversations, because you can learn to say things like, "I've noticed that your friend Jamie hasn't called you lately." If your teenager says yeah, you can say "I know you used to be such good friends. Is that hard for you? I'd like to understand what happened because you were very close for a while."

When you do this you will show a real awareness of and interest in your teenager's life.

FOURTH STEP

This next step is difficult for anyone who lives at the hectic pace that has become the norm for most of us. Working parents, parents with several children, or simply adults with their own complex lives find it a real challenge just to keep the practical aspects of family life under control. Every day you are faced with new situations that demand your attention.

Yet, through all this, you need to learn to show a sustained interest in your teenager by remembering to follow up on issues of interest or importance to him or her. For example, you might say, "I remember that you were really excited about going to that concert. Did it turn out to be as good as you hoped? How was the band?" This detailed, personal remark is quite different from saying, "How was the concert?" or not saying anything at all.

When parents show teenagers that they remember what matters to them and they ask relevant questions, it really lets them know that they are seen as individuals and that parents are interested in their lives.

FIFTH STEP

Your teenager may think that it's weird when you show such a personal interest, so you need to be prepared for a variety of responses. Some may even be positive! However, if your teenager doesn't respond positively by launching into a detailed conversation, don't get defensive or give up.

Say, "The way I'm talking to you may seem strange, but I really want us to have better conversations. I don't think that I always show you the kind of interest that I really feel about the things that happen in your life. You're important to me, so I hope you can get used to my questions. If they bug you, let me know. I don't want to intrude if you don't want to talk." This shows your respect for your kid's right to privacy. Try not to take it personally if you get no response.

SIXTH STEP

If you are honest with yourself, you may be thinking that you can't fake an interest in the things teenagers do. It just seems like a waste of time compared to adult concerns. I don't expect you to talk to your teenager like this all the time, but even if you make this effort once in a while, it can create a more positive, understanding relationship between you and your teenager.

Special Time with Your Teenager

Most parents think of special time as something that they do with younger children, but it can be a very valuable pursuit for you and your teenager. Some of you are probably thinking, He can't be serious! Special time means that once a week for ten minutes we yell at each other! My teen wants to spend time with me about as often as it rains in the Sahara desert! The only time the kids hang around is when they need money or when they need a ride somewhere. Hell, I get more rejection from my kids in a month than I experienced in all my years of dating! Special time? No, thanks!

Sounds like I'll have to work at convincing you about the importance of sharing a special time with your teenager.

When kids are younger, having a regular time with a parent during which they play a board game, read stories, or make models is very important. Children really look forward to that uninterrupted time with Mom or Dad, but as they get older they don't ask for or appear to need it as much, and so it's forgotten. Sure, they can survive without it, yet those meaningful moments can be very nourishing and comforting to a teenager who is struggling with giving up childhood, and they can have a lifelong effect.

Because most teenagers are very active and adult life is rarely leisurely, it's easy to let time pass without spending uninterrupted time alone with your teenager. One way to develop a better relationship or to deepen the one that you have is to suggest that you do something together once a month. This is a one-to-one activity that is different from the things that the whole family does together. During this time you can have each other's undivided attention. No phone calls, sibling rivalry, or household chores to spoil the fun. The idea is just to enjoy yourselves as you probably did when your child was little.

If you never had special time with your child, this would be a great time to start because it could lay the groundwork for a more adult relationship. Special time gives you a chance to keep in touch with the adult your teenager is becoming and spend meaningful time together before it is consumed by college, jobs, relationships, and careers.

FIRST STEP

Set up a time once a month or more often to do some activity that both of you will enjoy. If you want this effort to succeed, use some good judgment in choosing the activity. Don't suggest something that you can't stand just to get your kid to cooperate. It may end up being special for your teenager, but you'll wish you had never suggested it and will probably never do it again.

Likewise, doing something grown-up, meaning something that you like, can also be death to the experiment. Focus on mutually enjoyable activities such as dinner, a film, a sporting event, or cultural performance.

If there is more than one child in the family, parents can trade off. Remember, this is a leisure-time activity for enjoying each other's company. Don't use this time to discuss your teenager's problems, such as grades, unless he or she brings it up.

SECOND STEP

Even if your teenager doesn't respond well to your suggestion, try not to take this as personal rejection. Some teenagers will react very positively and others will be lukewarm. Your teenager may feel ambivalent about trying to fit you into a busy schedule or he or she may wonder if it'll feel uncomfortable trying to converse with you. He or she may even be suspicious about your real intentions. Is this just your way of getting a chance to deliver a lecture?

Say, "We're all really busy people, but I miss having time with you. I really would like it if we could do something special together once a month. It could be fun, so please think about it. It's okay if you're not sure about it right now. We can talk about it again. I'm not going to give up easily, because I really want to have some time with you."

Remember that no matter how awkwardly your teenager responds, your interest will probably feel flattering, and he or she could learn to enjoy the relationship with you through simple, regular activities.

THIRD STEP

If your teenager rejects this idea, say, "I hope someday you will think that this is a good idea and we can try it then. But even if you never want to do it, I'll understand and it's okay. You're still my kid and I love you even if we don't have much time together."

This says that you can accept your teenager's right not to spend time with you and still continue to love him or her. I know this may hurt, but it maintains a feeling of understanding between you. Don't conclude that your kid is a selfish brat. It just means that he or she is growing up.

Teenagers and Their Music

"Turn that music down! Even if you don't care about your eardrums, I'd like to preserve mine. How can you listen to such junk? If you'd memorize your schoolwork as thoroughly as those insipid lyrics, you'd be an A student." Frustrated parents may begin to believe that rock music does contain subliminal messages that scramble teenagers' impressionable brains and contribute to moral decline.

Observing teenagers in the grip of their favorite music, it is often difficult to tell if they are having a seizure and need the paramedics or if they've developed a terrific rash from head to toe; as if they are transported by the lyrics and decibels, they are in a world of their own—but unfortunately that world isn't soundproofed.

Headphones could solve many of the problems in the audio war, but teenagers prefer music that blasts out of their rooms, cascades down the stairs into the front yard, and rumbles through the neighborhood. Their justification is simple: It sounds better that way.

Many teenagers choreograph their lives to the sound of their favorite music. They seem to require music to pry themselves out of bed in the morning and fall asleep to a beat that sends most parents searching for aspirin or a more powerful pain reliever. This dependence on musical accompaniment extends to driving in the car—your car! Teenagers love the feeling of riding in a car that shudders from the bass line of a popular tape. Desperate parents long for earplugs, ejection seats, or vandals who will steal the sound system and end their slavery.

Teenagers have also discovered that portable music is an ingenious way to terrorize the general public. Carrying radios the size of air-conditioning units, they leave people cowering in doorways, hands pressed to their ears.

Hearing their loud, unrelenting, unintelligible music is one of the surest methods for making parents feel alienated from their teenagers. More than one harassed parent has suggested mandatory deportation of all thirteen-year-olds, with repatriation at twenty-one! So what do you do? Unfortunately, you can't do anything about all the other teenagers who pollute the airwaves, but you can exert some control over your own teenager's music behavior.

FIRST STEP

Think about your own listening habits. Maybe you are addicted to classical music or insist on hearing every financial report from six to nine in the evening. Perhaps silence is the sound you like best. Try to realize that everyone has a most comfortable style and volume of sound. Yours is probably different from your teenager's, and he or she needs to understand that as well.

Tell your teenager, "I realize that your music is really important to you, but we have very different taste in music. I am trying to make you understand that it is impossible for me to appreciate your music the way you do. I will try to stop yelling at you to turn down your music, but we need to have an understanding about how often and how loud you may play it."

SECOND STEP

Begin to negotiate with your teenager by saying, "I would like you to tell me a way that we can have a reasonable agreement about your music in this house. I realize that this might annoy you, but you need to think of some ways that will make playing your music more acceptable to us."

Your teenager may hit on a reasonable idea, such as using headsets when the family is home. If there are any complaints from the neighbors about the noise when you are not at home, then it'll have to be headsets all the time.

If teen's solution seems feasible, tell him or her that you will try the idea for a month. If it handles the noise problem consistently, you'll live with that solution.

THIRD STEP

If your teenager fails to follow his or her part of the agreement, say, "Our agreement about your music isn't working. So from now on you will have to agree to the following rules about playing music in the house. If your music is disturbing us, I will tell you once to turn it down or off. If you don't listen to me, I'll come into your room and stay until you turn it down. I'd prefer not to do that, but I will if the music continues to be a problem."

FOURTH STEP

If you have a teenager who continues to ignore the rules about playing music, or who lets music continually interfere with homework, chores, or family routines, this is the next step. Say, "From now on if your music prevents you from doing your homework or chores, you won't be allowed to listen to music for the rest of the day. If that doesn't seem to improve the situation, you will lose your music for longer and longer periods of time."

Remember that you increase the consequence until the undesirable behavior decreases.

If you have a teenager who listens to lots of music but is quite responsible, let him or her listen to it so long as he or she is considerate of your requests and it doesn't interfere with the life of the family. This issue should rarely become a major problem between you and your teenager. Try to think of it this way: If the worst thing your kid does is play music too loud or too long, you're in great shape!

Procrastination

Why does it seem biologically impossible for teenagers to do anything ahead of time? Did someone make a law that they must wait until the last minute and then panic and drag their parents into their trauma? Is procrastination a teenage plague, and is there a cure?

Parents are mystified and frustrated by kids who can get straight A's but wait until the day before the deadline to fill out college applications. "By the way, Dad, could you give me a complete financial statement with W-4s from the past three years, by tomorrow morning?" The wise teenager usually hides behind a door or a sturdy piece of furniture when delivering this type of request.

Parents recite a litany of warnings and questions, hoping to break the back of the procrastination beast. "You'd better get started writing that report." "Did you pick up your application for that job?" "Did you get that part for your car?" "Did you?" "Did you?" "Did you?" The parents' vocabulary seems to shrink to those two words as they try to nag their teenager into maturity.

The teenager's reaction is "Get off my case!" "Leave me alone!" "I said I'd do it!" and "God, you're the biggest nag!" When all their protests fail to produce any activity, parents announce in a satisfied tone, "I told you this would happen. Now will you listen to me the next time? You're never going to learn!"

Parents are infuriated by the fact that their kid can make elaborate preparations for special outings, down to the last detail, but draws a blank when they ask if the chores are done. One mother recently described her worst fantasy about her procrastinating teen: "I feel like I'll have to follow him around even after he's married to make sure he pays the bills on time." That's how maddening this issue can become for parents.

Concerned parents fear that their teenager will never learn to be responsible and handle his or her life. The teenager's agenda is to learn about responsibility slowly—still wanting to be a little kid though sometimes anxious to be grown-up. The little kid in the teen procrastinates.

Although procrastination is a part of normal development, that doesn't mean you can't help your teenager learn to show better control over this maddening behavior.

FIRST STEP

Observe your own behavior when you are trying to overcome your teenager's procrastination. Do you nag, check for progress, nag again, and finally threaten? Or do you fall into the role of rescuer? Does your kid leave an assignment until the last minute and then ask you for help, knowing that you just can't say no? So you stay up until two o'clock in the morning writing a report on the Civil War, and she nods off at midnight!

If this is your pattern, you must accept that you are a big part of the problem. You've taught your teenager that no matter how much he or she procrastinates, you'll be there to act as a one-person rescue team. So why would he or she be motivated to change?

SECOND STEP

Tell your teenager, "You really seem to have trouble getting things done in advance. At the last minute you panic and we all get upset. I need you to learn to be better organized and get things done on time. Can you think of any way to solve this problem?"

As in other issues, if your teenager arrives at a reasonable solution, agree to try it for a few weeks and then evaluate any progress. If the procrastinating continues to be an issue, move to the next step.

THIRD STEP

Tell your teenager, "I'm not going to take care of things for you when you procrastinate and get yourself into a bind. From now on you will have to learn to solve some problems in your own way. If you want me to help you with something and you wait until the last minute to ask me, I'm not going to do it. Please try to understand that I'm not doing this to be hard on you. But you have to learn to be more responsible about planning in advance."

FOURTH STEP

Tell your teenager, "I am not going to nag you anymore to see that you get things done on time. That just upsets both of us. Since you are still having problems with procrastinating, from now on you will have to do things when I ask you or within a reasonable amount of time." For example, if certain chores or academic tasks aren't completed by Friday, your teenager won't be able to go out with friends.

Being specific about the time and day on which you expect tasks to be completed gives your teenager freedom to schedule the tasks when she wishes, and informs her of the consequences of not acting responsibly. If the situation doesn't improve, increase the consequences to exclude other social activities including telephone calls and having friends over. Say, "I really hope that you will learn to follow these rules so that you don't have to lose all of your social activities."

FIFTH STEP

If you have a teenager who has a severe problem with procrastination, it is possible that none of your efforts affect the response because he or she doesn't care what you take away. In this case, you will need to use the approach suitable for a much younger child. Say, "I think it is very important that you learn to do things when they need to be done. This will be more and more important as you get older. From now on, if I find out that you haven't completed things that need to be done, I will make you stop whatever you are doing until they are done. I will make sure that you do it, even if it makes you mad."

For example, if your teenager hasn't started a report that is due, make him or her stop any other activity and say that the report is the only thing that he or she can do. Be a good observer. See that your teen is really working, and check every fifteen minutes.

Remember, if you want your teenager to stop procrastinating you must prove that you will not let anything interfere with follow-through. Your teenager is likely to get angry and frustrated, but try not to react to this. Say that until you see follow-through, it will seem like you are doing a lot of nagging. A typical statement might be: "I would prefer to leave things up to you, but until you can get things done when they are expected, you will have to get used to me interrupting whatever else you are doing." You are showing your teenager that you are taking absolute control until the procrastination improves.

This might really annoy your teenager, but it will make the point that severe procrastination has to stop. Remember to say, "Anytime you let me know that you're ready to be responsible without my supervision, I will be glad to stop." Praise even the smallest signs of improvement.

8

IF YOUR TEENAGER NEEDS
PROFESSIONAL HELP

"Please don't make me go to a shrink!"

Most normal teenagers will have days or even weeks in which they seem impossible, but then their behavior generally calms down and you are back to facing the everyday problems I have discussed in this book. They will have months of stable behavior but continue to need help with day-to-day issues.

Some parents reading this may be wondering if their teenager needs more help than they and this book can offer, and this can be a very upsetting thought. Just thinking about seeking professional help raises disturbing questions that most of us would rather avoid. "Is her life ruined?" "Can anything help him now?" "Is it my fault?" "Was I a good-enough parent?" Many parents respond to these questions by waiting and hoping that the problem will go away. It usually doesn't, and problems often get much worse while everyone is looking the other way. But I know that it can be very difficult to admit that the situation is so serious that professional help is needed.

Another reason parents are reluctant to seek professional help is that they anticipate resistance from their teenager. Few teenagers jump for joy at the idea of going to a shrink. Many feel that their parents are saying that they are sick, weird, or crazy if they need professional help. Parents are sensitive to these negative stereotypes and are very reluctant to force their kids to get help.

Once parents decide to investigate the possibility of getting professional help for their teenager, several important questions arise.

- How do I know when my teen needs professional help?
- What kind of therapy should I consider?
- What questions should I ask the therapist?
- How do I talk to my teenager about getting help?

Let's look carefully at each of these questions and try to relieve some of the anxiety that naturally arises around this very important issue. First, let's talk about the symptoms or patterns of behavior that suggest that your teenager may need professional help.

When to Seek Help?

As I have mentioned throughout this book, all teenagers have problems maturing and adjusting to the expectations of adulthood. All teenagers go through difficult periods when they are confused, withdrawn, or just cranky. Although these periods may be upsetting to both teenagers and their parents, they are not in themselves indications that a professional consultation is needed.

Two important indications that a problem requires professional intervention are *severity* and *persistence*. A problem is considered severe if it significantly disrupts your teenager's ability to function socially or scholastically, or if it disrupts the life of the family in a major way. Persistence indicates a problem that is present and must be dealt with for months at a time with little or no relief.

Changes in Behavior

1. Eating disorders, particularly loss of appetite.
2. Sleeping disorders, especially insomnia or the need for unusually long periods of sleep.
3. A pervasively negative view of life.
4. Persistent and almost constant unhappiness.
5. Loss of interest in things that were formerly important, such as music, sports, studies, and friends.
6. Withdrawal from social activities for long periods of time.

7. Withdrawal from the family, wanting seclusion, reluctance to talk.
8. Worrying excessively about life or the future.

Antisocial Behavior

1. Antisocial behavior, such as persistent lying or stealing.
2. Serious and frequent substance abuse.
3. Persistent argumentativeness, irritability, or anger.
4. Consistent disregard for rules and requests of parents or other authority figures.

If any of these patterns and attitudes persist over a three-month period and then stop but recur for periods of three to six months, it is a signal that your teenager is struggling with important issues that should be evaluated by a professional.

Thus far I have only discussed the symptoms in your teenager that indicate help should be considered. But another reason to seek help is if you find that you as a parent are acting inappropriately. You may have noticed that you overreact to minor issues with your teenager. If you are persistently frustrated, angry, or irritable for periods of up to three months and find that this is a recurring pattern, you should think about your need for help in understanding teenagers and parenting more effectively.

Even if you don't overreact but find that you are preoccupied about problems with your teenager, spend a lot of time thinking about issues and then rethinking them all over again, this may be an indication that things are not getting resolved. Talking with a therapist may help you clarify the source of the problems. In many cases it is not necessary to go into intensive therapy for yourself but to find a therapist who will focus primarily on problem-solving techniques.

These are not absolute guidelines but are simply ways to begin to evaluate your situation and the possible need for professional assistance.

What Kind of Therapy?

Once parents have decided that professional help would be appropriate and beneficial for their teenager, they are faced with the task of deciding what type of therapy would be best. My purpose in this section is to give some guidelines on the types of therapy that are available and discuss the most important treatment issues that must be considered when dealing with teenagers.

Therapy sessions are generally conducted in one of three general formats—individual, group, or family sessions or some combination of those three. The choice depends on the orientation of the therapist or clinic that you use. Some therapists prefer to work with teenagers alone in individual sessions. They may give little feedback to the parents and may suggest that parents find a therapist for themselves.

Other therapists believe that placing a teenager in a group with other teens is the most effective way to deal with their problem. Current thinking is that problems with teenagers should be treated in group sessions with as many family members as is appropriate. A therapist may also work with the teenager alone and then introduce family sessions.

Each approach has its strengths and limitations, which need to be carefully considered when choosing a therapist. Let's examine each more closely, beginning with individual therapy.

INDIVIDUAL THERAPY

Conducting therapy in individual sessions with teenagers assumes that the problems that are occurring can be solved simply by working with the teenager. This may give the message that the teenager's problems are unrelated to the attitudes and behavior of the parents. Although this approach can be effective, I believe that it is limited in value because some teenagers are not equipped to solve their own problems unilaterally just by talking to a therapist. Most of them need the parents' cooperation and help to change attitudes and interact differently.

There are a few exceptions to this point of view. If parents refuse to cooperate by being in therapy, individual sessions can provide a safe, positive, supportive experience for teenagers and can be the one place where they feel understood. Individual therapy can also be helpful for teenagers who get along well with their parents but have some specific anxiety or worry that they are reluctant to discuss with their parents. Talking with a therapist provides a safe environment for exploring opinions and ideas that are different from those of their parents. Some teenagers need to become comfortable in individual sessions before they are ready to talk in front of their parents.

GROUP THERAPY

Group therapy is a process that provides an opportunity for teenagers to compare feelings, attitudes, and values with other teens under the guidance of a trained professional. Group therapy can be very helpful for teens who don't have many friends and have difficulty relating to their peers. It can also be helpful for teens with limited social experience, because they can learn how other teenagers deal with problems that are similar to their own.

Sometimes group therapy is very effective because teenagers are confronted by their peers about inappropriate behavior concerning drugs, sex, or personal relationships. Being challenged by one's peers can have a much greater effect than listening to a dozen adult lectures. However, group therapy can't solve most of the family problems that are so prevalent during the teenage years because it only deals with the teenager.

FAMILY THERAPY

In my view, there are several reasons why family therapy is the most helpful approach for treating many teenage problems. The process of family therapy helps families recognize the inappropriate communication patterns that are causing problems for them and learn new ways to communicate with each other. This process helps families learn to listen to each other more effectively, to solve problems, and to compromise for the benefit of each member. It can teach people to understand and respect the feelings of other family members.

Family therapy can lessen the resistance that many teenagers feel about going to therapy because they won't have to go alone, feeling that they are the one with the problem. If the whole family attends sessions together, the message is that everyone has a part in the problem and everyone is responsible for helping to find a solution. Removing the stigma from the teenager generally lowers resistance and increases cooperation.

Second, family sessions help therapists to construct a more realistic picture of the total problem because, as they watch families interacting, they can see the part played by each person in the problem. Therapists can then help parents see their part in the problem and suggest ways to alter ineffective parenting patterns. Suggestions can be made for developing more positive approaches or attitudes toward problem areas.

A final advantage of family sessions is that it gives the therapist the opportunity to model new parenting techniques, which can substantially reduce routine problems with teenagers. Parents can try out these techniques and get some feedback in the safety of the therapist's office before using them at home.

In all my years of treating teenagers with problems, the most effective results have been achieved when family therapy is the treatment of choice or is part of the treatment approach.

How Do I Choose a Therapist?

Finding a competent professional in any field can be a challenge, but choosing a therapist can be a difficult and time-consuming task. A major concern is finding someone who is competent and can adequately treat the problems your teenager is having. Another consideration is finding someone with whom you feel comfortable discussing the problems and events of your personal life. Therapy is not easy, and the relationship between the therapist and client is a key factor in the ultimate success of the treatment.

Choosing a therapist with whom you can have a good working relationship is particularly difficult because the guidelines for making sound decisions are not clear. However, I believe that there are some procedures that you can use to assist you in finding the best possible help for your teenager and yourself. These include personal referrals, community resources, and interviews.

PERSONAL REFERRAL

For many people, the first choice in finding a therapist is to ask friends or professionals for a personal referral. In this case you would be looking for someone who had a good experience in therapy and would recommend the therapist without reservations. Of course, it is crucial that you respect the judgment and objectivity of the person making the referral. Sometimes your personal physician can be helpful in guiding you.

When inquiring, ask questions about the style of the therapist, the format of the sessions, personality, availability for emergencies, and any other issues that concern you. Asking questions is an essential part of the process of finding the right therapist.

COMMUNITY RESOURCES

If a reliable personal referral is not available, you must learn to use community resources for finding a therapist. In most communities the United Way has an information line, called INFO, which is a referral service for mental health services. Another excellent resource can be the psychology department of your local college or university. Academic institutions tend to have high standards for professional behavior and ethics and will generally make referrals to people or agencies that are known to be highly competent.

What to Ask the Therapist

Getting the name of a recommended therapist is only the first step in finding appropriate help for your teenager. Interviewing the therapist is the next important part of the process. There are several questions that you should ask your potential therapist the first time you make contact, whether it is on the phone or in a consultation meeting. Although you may feel a little intimidated about questioning professionals about their qualifications and methods, this is an essential aspect of getting effective therapeutic treatment.

Any therapist should be willing to respond to your questions openly. If the therapist has a positive attitude toward answering your questions, and you get clear and complete responses, that's an encouraging sign.

Begin by telling the therapist that you have a few questions you need to have answered before you can make a decision about working with him or her. Ask the following types of questions: "Would you mind telling me your background in working with teenagers?" "Do you have experience with family therapy?" "Are you experienced in teaching parents more effective parenting techniques?"

I feel that it is very important to choose a therapist who has strong training in working with teenagers and their families. At the risk of having thousands of therapists threaten to stone me, generally speaking I would discourage parents from seeing a therapist who lacked a significant amount of family therapy experience. I understand that there are some therapists who are able to work with teenagers even without training, but they would not be my first choice. If the therapist is going to work primarily with your teenager, ask how he or she usually consults with parents or keeps them informed of their child's progress without violating confidentiality.

A good sign for the parent is nondefensive attitude on the part of the therapist. A therapist should not try to convince you that he or she is right for you. Appropriate remarks would be, "I feel that with my background I can work with your son, but it's quite understandable of you want to think about it for a while or check with another therapist." "I really hear that you feel that you need a therapist who is flexible, and I think that is a very reasonable request." These remarks suggest willingness to hear the parents and be considerate of their feelings and needs.

Talking About Going to Therapy

Many teenagers feel that going to a "shrink" is an admission that something is wrong with them. "I'm not crazy! Why do I have to talk to a doctor?" Others feel very uncomfortable about discussing problems with anyone outside the family. "I'm not talking to a stranger about my personal life!"

Many teenagers have been threatened by frustrated parents, with the notion of going to a therapist, so it seems like a punishment for bad behavior rather than an attempt to help. "If you don't shape up, you're going to see a therapist because I'm fed up with you!" This type of introduction to the therapeutic process does nothing to encourage enthusiasm in teenagers with problems.

Even when you present the idea of going to therapy as constructively as possible, you are likely to encounter some resistance. Most teenagers struggle with accepting the idea that they need professional help, just as their parents do. They may feel that you think they are crazy or worry about what their friends will think if they find out. Many teenagers feel that it is embarrassing to talk about their problems with a stranger.

However, your attitude and approach can have a great influence on your teenager's eventual willingness to accept therapy. Be aware of your own attitude and anxieties about therapy before discussing it with your teenager. If you have negative feelings about therapy, your teenager may sense this and resist professional help even more.

FIRST STEP

In a calm moment, rather than during or right after a fight, tell your teenager, "I'm not sure how you will feel about this idea, but I want to suggest something that may help both of us. Since we have not been getting along, I would like us to go see a therapist. I'm not blaming you for the problems we're having. I think it's a family issue and we should all go. We need someone to help us get along better. We all have things to learn. It's not just you. I get too upset with you and you seem frustrated with me. I really want this to change."

If you teenager says, "I'm not going" or asks, "Why can't we just talk about our problems and try to settle it?" you need to tell him or her that there is no choice. Don't argue about this! Say, "I wish you felt differently about going but we still have to go. None of us is crazy. We just need some help. If I thought that we could solve our problems just by talking about them, I would gladly do it. But I need help with the way I am dealing with you."

SECOND STEP

Tell your teenager, "I have made an appointment, but I want to give you a choice. Would you rather go to the first meeting with the therapist alone or as a whole family? If you don't have a preference, we'll all go together." The purpose of this comment is to give your teenager some feeling of control.

THIRD STEP

Remember that many teenagers will continue to say that they are not going to therapy, no matter how positive you are. If that happens, allow your teen to verbalize displeasure and don't argue. This only encourages them to continue trying to change your mind. No matter what your teenager says, remember that you must make the decision about going to therapy based on your view of the situation, whether or not your teenager agrees.

FOURTH STEP

If your teenager says, "Okay, I'll go but I won't say anything!" don't scream, "At seventy-five dollars a shot, you'd better say something!" Try not to say, "You'd better not be rude when we go or you'll be grounded!" Instead say, "I realize this isn't something that you want to do, and if you don't want to say anything, that's all right. It might not be easy for any of us. But we need you to be there because all of us need to learn to get along better."

Don't argue about this issue with your teenager—he or she is really just expressing discomfort about being in therapy. A skillful therapist will be able to draw your teenager into the conversation, so don't worry about it.

FIFTH STEP

No matter how your teenager acts after the therapy session, don't ask if he or she liked it. That has a ring of "I told you so" and will immediately draw a negative response. Don't elaborate on how nice it is or try to convince your teen of its value. Accept his or her attitude, whatever it is, and work on being positive about the experience. Most teenagers will eventually accept the idea of therapy and may even learn to use it as a neutral place for solving problems.

CONCLUSION

Parents need to remember that the teenage years are the time when a child is progressing toward mastery of adulthood, with all its demands, responsibilities, challenges, and disappointments. So all those crazy things that your teenager does, apparently for the sheer pleasure of driving you up a wall, are actually part of learning to function independently and successfully in the adult environment.

It may help you to remember that your teenager's agenda is to act grown-up and be treated as an adult, even though he or she doesn't really feel ready for the adult world. This ambivalence causes a swing back and forth between very mature behavior, like getting a job, and very regressive tendencies, such as teasing a younger sister until she's in tears. During these retreats back to childhood your teen may seem so much younger than his or her actual years that you're convinced the kid'll never be mature enough to leave home. Of course, that's just about the time that he or she decides to act grown-up and capable again.

As parents, you need to develop a great deal of empathy for your teenager's passage from childhood to adulthood. It is a painful time in which children realize that they must give up the feeling that they can live forever as a kid in the safety of the family. They struggle with the inescapable separation anxiety that comes with this realization. Your teenager often feels like saying, "I don't want to be grown-up yet!

Why can't you take care of things for me?" This feeling accounts for much of the confusion and hesitation that accompany tasks such as choosing a college, applying for scholarships, or filling out job applications. The more all of these tasks remind your teenager that he or she isn't little anymore, the more his or her anxiety and ambivalence increase.

It takes great courage to face the loss of childhood and accept the inevitable responsibilities of functioning as an adult in the world. All teenagers are frightened by this challenge, yet excited about beginning life as an adult. Some will react to their fear by becoming inappropriately dependent, while others overreact and insist on handling everything without any adult assistance. But all teenagers need to know that their parents will always be there for them in some way, no matter how much they are out in the world. The transition to adulthood can be much less intimidating when you are understanding and empathic.

When teenagers mature in a healthy, supportive environment, they develop the confidence to trust their judgment and emotions rather than being overwhelmed by them, and to grapple with the challenge of becoming an adult.

When parents fail to discipline in a loving, firm, and effective manner, teenagers may not be able to develop an appropriate sense of separation that allows them to feel autonomous, independent, and secure about themselves. This leads to regressive behavior in which teens continue to feel insecure and treat the parents in a demanding, infantile manner, rather than developing mutual adult relationships.

If parents overindulge their teenager and fail to establish clear expectations about independence, he or she will remain tied to childish preoccupations and show little initiative concerning appropriate tasks and responsibilities. Overindulged teenagers may want to live at home and have all their needs met but object to having any responsibilities, in essence treating parents and other family members like servants. They have difficulty initiating a job search and need to be reminded repeatedly to complete any important tasks.

Teenagers need to be able to think independently and trust their own judgment. If parents squelch their teenager's autonomy by overdoing for them rather than letting them learn to be responsible for themselves in meaningful ways, their teenager will be unable to develop a sense of personal resources and will lack confidence in his or her ability to take care of and rely on him- or herself.

Teenagers who fail to master these skills continue to depend inappropriately on their parents because they feel that they can't depend on themselves. They become more and more frustrated, wanting to function like an adult yet feeling utterly unprepared for their future. These teenagers may demand the right to be trusted and protest that their parents shouldn't control their spending, yet continue to act irresponsibly about bills. They still need their parents' help to grow up but can't admit it because it makes them feel dependent. This can be the result of ineffective parenting.

However, even when parents do a very good job of parenting, some teenagers continue to struggle with the idea of functioning as a grown-up. Teenagers who are struggling with this challenge need firm, supportive parenting. Even though it may take them longer to grow up, eventually they will accept the idea that they are capable of managing their own lives.

Teenagers want to look at life with hope and optimism. No matter how worried you may be during your child's adolescence, it is important that you convey to your teenager a belief in his or her ability to have a meaningful life. Think about all that you did and experienced as a teenager, and yet you became a responsible, productive member of society. You must have faith that the same will be true of your child, no matter how difficult some adolescent issues have been. When teenagers grow up with the certainty that you believe in them, they gain a self-confidence that creates a real sense of pride in themselves and hope for the future.

Some of you may be thinking that now you know more about discipline, and the battles have been reduced to minor skirmishes, but you may be wondering if your kid will ever really like you. Take heart! As teenagers approach their twenties, they become less ambivalent about their parents and even begin to understand that their parents made demands and set limits because they cared about them. In other words, you are seen less as an ogre and more as the caring, responsible parent that you are trying to be. Your efforts to help your teenager mature will ultimately be seen as proof of the deep and abiding love that you have for your child.

FOR FURTHER READING

Publications

Bell, Ruth. *Talking with Your Teenager.* New York: Random House, 1984.

This book emphasizes communication skills, reflective listening without judgment, reading indirect behavioral communications, and parental self-awareness of inappropriate expectations. Encourages parental knowledge of special biological, social, emotional issues of teen years. Uses system of consequences for discipline.

Dinkmeyer, David and Gary McKay. *The S.T.E.P. Approach to Parenting Teenagers.* (American Guidance Service). New York: Random House, 1983.

This book concentrates on teaching the skills of reflective listening, exploring alternative courses of action with the teenager, understanding the underlying goal of the behavior, and determining who "owns the problem."

Elkind, David. *All Grown Up and No Place to Go—Teenagers in Crisis.* Reading, Mass.: Addison-Wesley, 1984.

Insightful view of pressures facing teenagers in a society that expects them to confront and cope with adult situations prematurely. Concentrates on educating parents to the dangers of stress on teenagers. This book is one that heightens parents' awareness of problems but does not offer practical advice on day-to-day issues.

Ellis, Albert and Robert A. Harper. *A New Guide to Rational Living.* Englewood Cliffs, N.J.: Prentice-Hall, 1975.

A solid book by the founder of rational counseling dealing with rational and irrational ways to think about life's issues.

196

Ginott, Haim. *Between Parent and Teenager.* New York: Macmillan, 1971.

This book endures on the bookshelves as a classic in the reflecting feelings approach, with emphasis on nonjudgmental communication and respect for the special issues of the teen years. Offers education on these issues and help for parents in clarifying their values, but little practical advice.

Herbert, Martin. *Living with Teenagers.* Basil Blackwell, 1987.

This is a book about coping with serious problems of teenagers, for example, drug abuse, alcoholism, and the like.

Johnson, Vernon E. *I'll Quit Tomorrow.* Rev. ed. New York: Harper & Row, 1980.

This is the basic book on the nature of alcoholism and its treatment by one of the pioneers in the field.

McCoy, Kathleen. *Coping with Teenage Depression.* New York: Penguin, 1985.

A comprehensive book on symptoms of depression vividly described. Helps parents recognize and finally accept the fact that even teenagers who seem to have everything can be seriously depressed. A valuable resource.

Nahas, Gabriel G. *Keep Off the Grass.* Oxford: Pergamon Press, 1979.

This is more a scholarly treatment of the history of attitudes toward marijuana in the United States, including the development of solid research indicating its danger.

Polson, Beth and Miller Newton. *Not My Kid. A Parent's Guide to Kids and Drugs.* New York: Avon, 1985.

A perceptive, practical book that shows parents how to identify a drug problem and what to do about it.

Shinley, Gould. *Teenagers, the Continued Challenge.* New York: Hawthorn, 1979.

A comprehensive book on teenage development and problems during this period of development.

York, Phyllis and David, and Ted Wachel. *Toughlove.* New York: Bantam Books, 1983.

This approach advocates a very active system of confrontation and intervention in combination with a parent-group and community-support system. The focus is on helping teens already in serious trouble with authority. Has limits for small day-to-day problems with teenagers.

Young, Bettie. *Helping Your Teenager Deal with Stress.* New York: St. Martin's Press, 1986.

A book that identifies stressful issues for teenagers and tells how to deal with stress during adolescence.

Resources

ALCOHOL AND DRUG ABUSE

1-800-Cocaine. Information and Hotline for Teenage Drug Users, 1-800-234-TEEN.

National Clearinghouse for Alcohol Information
P.O. Box 2345
Rockville, Md. 20853

> Write for list of alcohol treatment facilities and programs in your area and a free copy of *The Drinking Question: Honest Answers to Questions Teenagers Ask about Drinking.*

National Federation of Parents for Drug-free Youth
P.O. Box 57217
Washington, D.C. 20037

> Send for NFD starter kit with information on how to start a local parent group.

National Institute on Drug Abuse
P.O. Box 2305
Rockville, Md. 20852

> Ask for free books: *Parents, Peers and Pot* and *For Parents Only: What You Need to Know about Marijuana.*

Parent Resources and Information on Drug Education
PRIDE
Georgia State University
University Plaza
Atlanta, Ga. 30303

PARENT SUPPORT GROUPS

Al-Anon
World Service Office
P.O. Box 182
Madison Square Station
New York, N.Y. 10159
(212) 481-6565

> Al-Anon helps relatives of alcoholics learn to deal with the problem drinker more effectively and to make their own lives more manageable, whether or not the alcoholic stops drinking. You can usually find your local chapter in your telephone directory, but can get literature about the organization and the location of the group nearest you by writing to the above address.

Parents and Friends of Gays
P.O. Box 24528
Los Angeles, Calif. 90024

> You can write to this address for information about the group in your area. The reply will be confidential and arrive in a plain envelope.

Parents Anonymous
22330 Hawthorne Blvd., #208
Torrance, Calif. 90505

Hotline (crisis counseling and information available twenty-four hours a day, seven days a week):
California: (800) 352-0386
Outside California: (800) 421-0353

> Parents Anonymous is a national organization with more than 1,000 chapters in the United States. All services, which include working with volunteer professionals to solve problems with children and getting support in weekly meetings with professionals and other parents, are free.

Parental Stress Line
In Massachusetts: (800) 632-8188
Outside Massachusetts: (617) 742-7573

> This is a twenty-four-hour service for parents experiencing crises with their children. Out-of-state callers may ask for a referral to their local stress line.

Toughlove
Community Service Foundation
P.O. Box 70
Sellersville, Pa. 18960

> This program helps parents develop new strengths to give a sense of support and firm directions to troubled teens who may be acting out in school, or within the family, or having trouble with drugs, alcohol, or the law.

PARENTING EDUCATION

Parenting classes are sponsored by many community and national organizations such as the YMCA, Red Cross, and PTA, as well as private groups. These classes are designed to help clarify values, improve communication skills, and to help you in your efforts to understand and to set firm guidelines for your teenager.

To get more information on parenting courses, write to:

Effectiveness Training, Inc.
531 Steven Avenue
Solona Beach, Calif. 92075

> Ask for descriptive literature or location of the parenting effectiveness course nearest you.

Institute for Adolescent Studies
311 South San Gabriel Blvd.
Pasadena, Calif. 91107

You can write to this main office for the address of the institute in your area.

The Parent/Early Childhood and Special Programs Office
U.S. Department of Education
400 Maryland Avenue S.W.
Washington, D.C. 20202

PREGNANCY SERVICES FOR ADOLESCENTS

For abortion referral, check the white pages of your telephone directory for local listings of:

Clergy Counseling Service

Or call the National Abortion Federation Hotline at (800) 223-0618

National Organization for Women

Planned Parenthood

For alternatives to abortion, check the white pages of your telephone directory for local listings of:

Birthright

Children's Home Society (in California)

Florence Crittenden Association (or Crittenden Services)

Write to the following address for the group nearest you.

Parenting Support Group for Adolescents
National Association Concerned with School-Age Parents
7315 Wisconsin Avenue
Suite 211-W
Washington, D.C. 20014

THERAPY RESOURCES AND REFERRALS

If you're looking for a qualified family counselor, psychiatrist, or psychologist, you might seek referrals from professional organizations. Some of these include:

American Association for Marriage and Family Therapy
924 W. 9th Street
Upland, Calif. 91786
(714) 981-0888

This organization has more than 7,500 members in the United States and Canada. You can write or call for free referrals to qualified family counselors.

American Psychiatric Association
1700 18th Street N.W.
Washington, D.C. 20009
(202) 797-4900

American Psychological Association
1200 17th Street N.W.
Washington, D.C. 20036
(202) 833-7600

Family Service Association of America

The Family Service Association of America, with member agencies nationwide, offers low-cost individual and family counseling, family-life education programs, special rap groups for teens, and family advocacy activities.

Check the white pages of your local telephone directory for member agencies.

Info-Line

Referral and resource service in most cities funded by United Way.

INDEX

ABOUT THE AUTHORS

Don Fleming, Ph.D., author of *How to Stop the Battle with Your Child*, is a psychotherapist whose expertise lies in the areas of child and adolescent psychology. For more than thirty years he has worked with parents and children, developing a unique approach to parenting that is practical, effective, and humorous. His experience with teenagers began early in his career, when he worked as a youth director specializing in programs for teenagers, and he refined his insights and techniques in his private practice. His wife, Pamela, attributes his success with teenagers to the fact that he is still half-teenager himself. He is the former director of training at the Julia Ann Singer Center in Los Angeles.

In addition to his private practice, Dr. Fleming writes for numerous periodicals and is a highly regarded speaker on the topic of child development. He has appeared on national television and is a frequent guest on the radio. He is currently working on several books and seminar projects.

Laurel J. Schmidt is a freelance writer, living in Los Angeles, who specializes in the areas of education and art. She is the coauthor of *Contemporary Art Start—A Guide to Contemporary Art for Children* and is currently an educational consultant at the Museum of Contemporary Art. Ms. Schmidt is also a language development specialist in the Los Angeles Unified School District.